LD

Books by Donald Day

Backwoods to Border
(Edited with Mody C. Boatright:
a Texas Folklore Society Publication)

From Hell to Breakfast
(Edited with Mody C. Boatright:
a Texas Folklore Society Publication)

Big Country: Texas
(American Folkways Series)

The Autobiography of Will Rogers
(Editor)

Franklin D. Roosevelt's Own Story
(Editor)

How We Elect Our Presidents (by Will Rogers)
(Editor)

Woodrow Wilson's Own Story
(Editor)

Uncle Sam's Uncle Josh, or, Josh Billings on Practically Everything
(Editor)

Uncle Sam's Uncle Josh

UNCLE SAM'S
Uncle Josh

or

Josh Billings on Practically Everything

Distilled from

JOSH'S RUM-AND-TANSY NEW ENGLAND WIT

by DONALD DAY

Next to William Shakespeare, Josh Billings is the greatest judge of human nature the world has ever seen.

— ABRAHAM LINCOLN

Boston
LITTLE, BROWN AND COMPANY

LIBRARY OF CONGRESS CATALOG CARD NO. 53-5263

FIRST EDITION

Published simultaneously
in Canada by McClelland and Stewart Limited

PRINTED IN THE UNITED STATES OF AMERICA

To

MARY W. *and* RALPH L. FEAGLES

Uncle Josh's Foreword

Americans love caustic things; they would prefer turpentine to cologne if they had to drink either.

So with their relish of humor; they must have it on the half shell with cayenne. If you tickle or convince an American you have got to do it — *quick!* He works, eats and haw-haws on a canter.

An Englishman wants his fun smothered deep in mint sauce, and he is willing to wait till next day before he tastes it.

I guess the English have more wit, and the Americans more humor. We haven't had time, yet, to boil down our humor and get the wit out of it.

Don't forget *one* thing: you have got to be wise before you can be witty; and don't forget *two* things: a single paragraph has made some men immortal while a volume has been worse to others than a pile driver.

I hope I have written something that will make the world better. I am so enamored of cheerfulness that I would like to live to be one hundred and nine years old, and be known, far and near, as that festive old cuss, Josh Billings.

Contents

Uncle Sam's Uncle Josh

CHAPTER ONE

Uncle Josh's Boyhood

"When I was a boy I was anxious to know as much as a man does, but now I am a man I wish I knew as little as a boy does."

Josh Billings was born Henry Wheeler Shaw on April 21, 1818, in Lanesboro, Massachusetts, at a time when the United States was shedding its pinfeathers for a self-conscious, croaking crow. She had whipped England for a second time, knew it "by gosh," and was already breaking through the mountains in great swarm preparatory to flowing in succeeding waves across the North American continent to the Pacific.

Baby Henry's pedigree had little rust on it. It was good solid New England ancestry with a conscious concept of an "early to bed, early to rise" duty both to do the job and to get the rewards (if God in his wisdom chose to allow it). Henry's paternal grandfather was a noted surgeon and his father a politician successful enough to get to Congress and to be a close friend of Henry Clay. Henry's mother came from well-to-do farmer stock that Jefferson would have hallelujah'd over to populate his agricultural utopia.

Lanesboro itself was peopled by industrious, God-fear-

ing, frugal men and women, who wouldn't sand their sugar or water their rum before selling it without praying first.

But all of this good influence could not keep Henry from being an indolent, trifling boy, who shirked his work to go trout fishing on the clear-water streams in the long line of blue hills that overlooked the little town, or to swim in Pontoosuc and Oneta lakes, or to climb the rugged sides of old Greylock.

There were other things that he liked to do that the deacons in the church might have, in spite of their own memories, objected to. Henry told about them later:

When I was a boy all kinds of juvenile cussedness was in full bloom and must have been at a premium. I can't look back and see that I was very malicious, but to say that I was at the head of my Sunday School class, or hankered hard for the catechism, would be saying too much.

I always went to school by the way of somebody's orchard and green apples and me was the best of friends, especially if they was hard to hook.

I learned to keep my eyes open and saw a lot of pretty things. Strawberries was one of them. The strawberry is one of nature's pets. Its color is like the setting sun under a thin cloud, with a delicate dash of the rainbow in it. Its fragrance is like the breath of a baby when it first begins to eat wintergreen lozenges; its flavor is like the nectar which an old-fashioned goddess used to leave in the bottom of her tumbler when Jupiter stood treat on Mount Ida.

I stole them, laying around loose, without any pedigree, in somebody's tall grass, when I was a lazy schoolboy, that ate dreadful easy, without any white sugar on them, and occasionally even a bug mixed with them in the hurry of the moment.

Cherries are good but they are too much like sucking a marble with a handle to it. Watermelons will suit anybody who is satisfied with half-sweetened drink; but the man who can eat strawberries, besprinkled with crushed sugar, and besmattered with sweet cream (at somebody else's expense) and not lay his hand on his stomach, and thank the author of strawberries and stomachs, is a man with a worn-out conscience—a man whose mouth tastes like a hole in the ground, that don't care what goes down it.

Peaches and cream will convert any boy who is worth saving. The peach has a down on it, like the down on a maiden's cheek, but it ain't half so pleasant to get onto the lips. Peach brandy is made out of the peach. This liquor has been called mellow, but it will lay out a saint just as flat as it will a sinner. I drank as a boy a teaspoon full of it warm from the still, and it was 20 minutes before I could draw a long breath. I was as hot inside as a chimney on fire, and I thought I would break out and blaze somewhere, but it didn't happen so.

Stealing watermelons on dark and rainy nights was a pious duty when I was a boy. Here's how we did it.

Sometime about the 20th of August, more or less, when the moon is entering her second quarter, and the old kitchen clock has struck twelve midnight, get up and dress yourself, without making any noise, and leave the house by the back door, and step lightly across the yard, out into the highway, and turn to your right.

After going about half a mile, take your first left-hand road, and when you come to a bridge, cross it, and go through a pair of bars on the right, walk about two hundred yards in a southeast direction, and you will come suddenly on a watermelon patch.

Pick out a good, dark-colored one, with the skin a little ruffled. Be careful not to injure any of the vines by stepping on them. Shoulder the watermelon and retrace your steps, walking about twice as fast as you did when you come out.

Once in a while look over your shoulder to see if the *moon* is all right. When you reach home, bury the watermelon in the hay mow and slip into bed, just as though nothing had happened.

This is the old-fashioned, time-honored way to pick out a good watermelon, just the way our fathers and grandfathers did it. But after you have et the watermelon tear up the receipt. I am not anxious to have it preserved, but I don't want it forgotten.

Tying two cats together by their tails and leaving them to pull and claw and fight it out on a clothesline was the fashion, when I was a boy, but I will take my oath on a Bible as big as a barn door that I never did it.

Hitching old and worm-eaten tinware to the opposite end of a vagrant canine, and losing sight of the poor animal for the dust he kicked up, as he frantically fled along the streets to the music of his own yells of terror, was another cruel scene in the comedy of boy deviltry, but I solemnly declare that I never hung any tin things to a dog's suburbs, according to the best of my remembering.

I trapped every winter for muskrats, and bought the first pair of skates I ever owned with their skins. I have seen them in the winter setting upon end on the ice, close beside their holes as stiff as an exclamation point, and when they saw me they'd change ends and point down, like a semicolon, and that was the last of them.

I loved to go fooling around among the animals of all kinds on a warm day. I still had rather set down by the side of an anthill and see the whole swarm pitch onto a lazy cuss who won't work and run him out of the diggings, than to set 6 hours at the opera and applaud what I don't understand, and weep at the spot where the rest do, and pay 3 dollars for the privilege of doing it.

Study nature and you will find out where all the truth comes from. Natural history is dog cheap.

To open our eyes and think while we are looking is all the capital necessary for the naturalizing business.

Book education is a fatting thing. It makes a man stick out with other folks' opinions and is a good thing to make the vulgar roll up the whites of their eyes and wonder how any man could ever know so much wisdom.

Schooling, when I was a colt, didn't lie around so loose as it does now, and learning was picked up oftener by running your head against a stone wall than by any other kind of mineralogy.

I have studied botany all day, in a flat meadow, pulling cowslips for greens, and then classified them, by picking them over and getting them ready for the pot.

All the astronomy I ever got I learnt in spearing suckers by moonlight, and my geology culminated at the further end of a woodchuck's hole, especially if I got the woodchuck.

As for moral philosophy and rhetoric, if it is the science of hooking green apples and watermelons 30 years ago, and being awful sorry for it now, I am up head in that class.

But if I don't remember my schooling in books, I remember my schoolteachers — with sadness.

I have never yet known a country schoolmarm to be over twenty-three years old. She remains right there for an indefinite period of time. She wears her hair either cut short or hanging in ringlets, and is as prim and precise in everything as a pair of platform scales. She seldom ever smiles and was never known to laugh out loud; but when she does, she does it according to the rules laid down by Murray for speaking and pronouncing the English language correctly. It must be just so.

She is a paragon of propriety and had rather be three years behind in styles than to spell one word wrong or to parse a sentence incorrectly. I never knew one to die an old maid. She generally marries some fellow who has less education than she has and he thinks she's the smartest thing that ever walked on top of this green earth. Why, Noah Webster is not in it, and old man Ben Franklin has to take a back seat. With all her concise foibles and idiosyncrasies, I have always had a tender spot in my heart for her. She is stepmother to more bad boys' children than anybody else and has the patience and forbearance of Job with naughty boys and stupid girls. May heaven's richest and choicest blessings lie upon her and abide with her. She works the hardest and gets the nearest to no pay for it of any person I know in a civilized and Christian land.

And there is one man in this world to whom I always take off my hat and remain uncovered until he gets safely by, and that is the schoolmaster.

When I meet him I look upon him as a martyr just returning from the stake, or on his way there to be cooked. He leads a more lonesome and single life than an old bachelor, and a more anxious one than an old maid. He is remembered just about as long and as affectionately as a guide board is by a traveling pack peddler.

If he undertakes to make his scholars love him, the chances are he will neglect their learning, and if he don't lick them now and then, pretty often, they will soon lick him.

The schoolmaster ain't got a friend on the flat side of the earth. The boys snowball him during recess; the girls put water in his hair dye; and the school committee makes him work for half the money a bartender gets and board him around the neighborhood where they give him rye coffee, sweetened with molasses to drink, and codfish balls 3 times a day for vittles.

Don't talk to me about the patience of ancient Job. Job had pretty plenty of boils all over him, no doubt, but they were all of one breed. Every young one in a school is a boil of a different breed, and each one needs a different kind of poultice to get a good head on them.

Why is it that these men and women, who patiently and with crazed brain teach our remorseless brats the tedious meaning of the alphabet, who take the first welding heat on their destinies, who lay the stepping stones and encourage them to mount upwards, who have done more hard and mean work than any class on the footstool, who have prayed over the reprobate, strengthened the timid, restrained the outrageous, and flattered the imbecile, who have lived on codfish and vile coffee, and ain't been heard to swear — why is it that they are treated like a vagrant fiddler, danced to for the night, paid off in the morning, and eagerly forgotten?

I had rather burn a coalpit or keep the flies out of a butcher's shop in the month of August than meddle with the district school business.

After learning his three R's in a district school, Henry was sent to a school at Lenox, a few miles from Lanesboro, to prepare for college. Although it can not be said that he loved to study, he did relish Virgil more than the chores around a farm. Nor can it be said that he followed his teacher's precept: "Whatever you get, get it got."

He did, however, pick up enough information to get

admitted to Hamilton College, a Presbyterian institution at Clinton, nine miles southwest of Utica, New York. But his love for pranks far outshone his fondness for learning, and his love of wandering in the countryside, fishing and just observing, exceeded even his joy from practical jokes. So it is a wonder that he scraped by his freshman year.

On his return the next fall — by a roundabout way on steamboats and stagecoaches, to delay his getting there — he heard exciting tales of the great West. Things were happening out there that were calling to red blood — things that would make Horace Greeley's "Go West, young man," an aphorism instead of a banishment.

Back in Hamilton, living in a room that faced the chapel, Henry was awakened each morning by a bell that called all students to religious service. For Henry it may have been opportunity ringing. One morning before the bell got in its peals, Henry shinnied up a lightning rod (which is still on the chapel) and removed the clapper from the bell. The President of the College promptly removed Henry from the campus.

Back home Henry was neither an ornament to his family nor a joy to himself. He did a few odd chores around the house; read deeply in Shakespeare; and spent the rest of his time longing to go West.

"I guess you had better go," his father said one day. "You certainly aren't doing any good around here."

So he gave the boy a ten-dollar bill, his mother fixed him a bundle of clothes, and off he went, not to come back for ten years.

CHAPTER TWO

Uncle Josh Went West

"Thrice armed is he that hath his quarrel just
And four times he who gets his fist in fust."

The ten dollars lasted Henry until he got across the state of Illinois. Then he was on his own. By doing odd jobs he worked his way to St. Louis which by this time (probably 1835) was already the metropolis of the Southwest. Henry wandered up and down the waterfront and soon struck up an acquaintance with a band of adventurous youths all of whom wanted to cross the plains and explore the Rocky Mountains. From there they eagerly planned a trip on further west or down into Mexico. Among them was a young German geologist and a couple of Canadian voyageurs.

Henry, armed with letters which his father had secured from ex-President John Quincy Adams, Henry Clay and Martin Van Buren, was elected leader of the party.

The expedition took several weeks to cross the state of Missouri, following the Missouri River, and then headed across Kansas. When the young adventurers reached a place which is about where Topeka, Kansas, now stands, fever broke out. The German geologist died and was buried on the prairie. Food became scarce and marauding Indians plentiful. The survivors straggled back to St. Louis.

Sometime later, as Josh, Henry claimed to have gotten down into Arkansas where, upon hearing a weird, strange noise, he found a violin so large that it took a couple of oxen to draw the bow across it. When the man playing it wanted to change the notes he simply geed and hawed to his yoke of oxen.

Of course Henry might have heard of this Bunyanesque musical instrument in St. Louis, but the important thing is, as Frank Dobie has so well put it, that he might have seen it. The great American frontier produced some marvelous things before written records reduced them to size.

From St. Louis, Henry took wing for Toledo, Ohio, where he joined forces with a couple of other kindred spirits, Gideon Weed and Josh Carew. Like Henry they were too full of wild frolic and fun to meddle much with business. Their first foray was a trip up the Maumee River to see what adventures they might uncover. At an inn in Napoleon, Ohio, they found themselves without a penny and with a thirst and hunger. Something had to be done to replenish the exchequer.

At that time the country was excited over mesmerism. The three boys, getting their heads together, decided to give a lecture on mesmerism enlivened with other fun. It was determined that Gideon should write a skit on the subject, Henry would deliver it as a lecture, and Josh would sing comic songs. Their handwritten announcements read:

MORDECAI DAVID

The last surviving relative of David, the original author of the David Psalter, will read a

LECTURE ON MESMERISM

to the citizens of Napoleon on

FRIDAY NIGHT

And the lecture will be prefaced by some characteristic songs by

OTTO HAYWOOD

the sweet singer from the East.

By lecture time Friday night the little parlor of the inn was crowded to capacity. Henry was well over six feet, rangy, and wore his black hair long, down over his shoulders to hide a birthmark. He had on a wide-brimmed sombrero which added to his dignity. Talking in a serious solemn manner, a natural mimic, he kept the audience in an uproar. "The sweet singer from the East" further delighted them. The take was $13.40 — equal to about two hundred dollars in our money.

There was much talk around the inn and on the steets of Napoleon about a return engagement a week later. But Henry solemnly advised against it. Being a confirmed practical joker himself, he just wasn't certain whether the interest was in another program or if the elfish spirits in Napoleon might be planning something more physical and less psychic than mesmerism.

Sometime in his wanderings, Henry spent a year or longer at Norwalk, Ohio, a pleasant little town fifty miles southwest of Cleveland. Out of money (as usual) he took a job as office boy for the legal firm of Boalt & Worcester. He was, he said, interested in the study of the law. But he did more wandering about the countryside than he did office-boying or plunging into Blackstone. Mr. Boalt met him one day on the street.

"I haven't seen you in the office much lately, Henry," he said.

"The office must have moved," Henry replied solemnly, "I haven't been able to find it."

Henry tried his hand at horse trading in Norwalk. In general he may have come out ahead but on one occasion he didn't. He had an old pelter that he wanted to get rid of. The other man had his horse in front of Henry's boardinghouse, where there was a deep ditch. Henry closed out a mite too fast. When he started to lead his horse away, out of this ditch, where he hadn't seen it, came a great deformed foot.

He was more successful in his pranks. At that time the Millerites, a sect that believed the end of the world was at hand, were preparing more to go to Heaven than for their stay on earth. One evening as the preacher was letting his congregation have his heaviest artillery, a long boat hook came in from a window back of him, caught him in the seat of the trousers, and out he went. For a moment the congregation thought the end of the world had come and that their leader was making his ascension.

The suspicion generally held in Norwalk was that

Henry was at the other end of that hook. Later, as Josh, he wrote something that is at least good circumstantial evidence, considering his love for pranks as primary:

The second adventists, and adventisses, are a people of slow growth, but remarkable vigor and great endurance. They have been to work, with both hands, for about thirty years in bringing this world to her milk; and though often outfigured in the arithmetic of events, they rub out the slate and begin again.

Like all other moral enthusiasts for right or wrong, they tap the Bible for their nourishment, and several times, so they say, have only missed in their calculations but about two inches — which is mighty close for so big a thing.

The time has been sot, at least a dozen times since I have been an inhabitant in this country, and when I was a boy, as tender and as green as celery, I can recollect of having awful palpitations in the neighborhood of the kneepans, upon one of those eventful days, and crawled under the barn, not to be in the way.

But as I grew older, I come to the conclusion, some time since, that Divine Providence created the world, without any of the succor or scientific attainments of man, and He probably would be able to destroy it in the same way.

I have always thought, judging from what little I have been able to pick, that was lying aound loose, of man's internal nature, that if the world hadn't been built, before man was, he probably wouldn't have been satisfied if he couldn't have put in his lip.

Man is an uneasy critter, and loves to tell how things ought to be built and has got just impudence enough to offer his valuable services to the Lord, especially in the way of advice.

Now I am confidently of the opinion that the world will sometime be knocked out of time; it ain't got the least particle of immortality about it, that I have been able to discover. It is as certain to die as man is, and I think anybody who will take a slate and pencil and straddle a chair calmly and cipher out the earth's death to a day, is no wiser, nor less imprudent and wicked, than if he figgered on his neighbor's funeral and then blabbed it around town.

I don't know whether Mr. Miller was the inventor of this second advent abortion or not, but if he was, I will bet a half pint of peanuts, and pay whether I win or lose, that he was a fat, lazy old simpleton who lived on a back road, as ignorant of the Bible as a country horse doctor is of medicine.

My opinion is if the world should consent to come to an end, to suit their reckoning, they would be as scared a set of carpetbaggers as you could find, and be the first ones to say that the figgers lied.

I am willing to double my half pint bet of peanuts, and make it a pint, that there ain't a Millerite now living, nor ever a-going to live, whom you could get to take 87½ cents in change for a dollar greenback, or who would give a double price for breakfast, on the morning of the day that is sot for the world's destruction.

Enthusiasm, and second adventism, is cheap, but a dollar is worth the face of it.

Somehow I suspect from reading this that Henry did not have the same sympathy for this sort of a humbug that he did for a dog. But after all, a boat hook in the seat of the pants, followed by a premature ascension, is about as bad as a bit of tinware to a dog's tail. Especially when it was followed a few weeks later by the firing off of a cannon which caused the congregation to rush outside thinking the end of the world had come — only to find they had been made the victims of another joke. It has been said that Henry lit the fuse to that shot, but the men who go on to fame get credit for doing a lot of devilment they didn't do and credit for doing a lot of good that they didn't do also.

Out of funds again, this time in Norwalk, Henry, through the local newspaper, announced a lecture on "Milk." The local bucolics filled the hall to capacity, expecting to get new ideas on the production of milk. But after talking for half an hour, without bringing up the subject, Henry asked, "Does anyone want to ask a question?"

"Yes," said a bewhiskered old patriarch with a belligerent gleam in his eyes, "you spoke on everything under the sun except milk. I want to know about that."

"Why," said Shaw, with his most winning smile, "I

drank a quart of milk before I mounted the platform. Of course I have been lecturing on *milk."*

An ominous growl went up from the audience which was quickly drowned by roar after roar of laughter. Henry, whose eyes had explored the size of a window back of him, then went on to give them more of his witticisms.

What Henry did in these few places, which in his writings he gives tracks of, will have to serve as examples of what he did in the entire ten years. Nothing else has been uncovered. In 1845 he returned home, now twenty-seven years of age, without money or position, but definitely having seen how the other side of the mountains lived. He later wrote:

Wild oats are a natural grain to the soil of man, as natural as measles, and while at all times there is more or less danger in raising the crop, those who sow early and sow plentiful are the safest.

CHAPTER THREE

Uncle Josh "Jumps the Broomstick"

"Marrying for love may be a little risky but it is so honest that God can't help but smile on it."

Henry was surprised, and pleased, on his return to Massachusetts, to find that his childhood sweetheart, Zilpha Bradford, had not yet married. He lost no time in convincing her that he was her man. They got married in typical Shaw fashion. The state laws required that the banns be published for three consecutive Sundays. To avoid this, they drove in a buggy to Lebanon, New York, twelve miles away, and were married without waiting. Those who knew Henry best said he was avoiding a just punishment for what he had helped do to other couples less discreet. "Those who love to play jokes the most on others," he later confessed, "love least to have jokes played on them."

As Josh he had much to say on marriage:

An old bachelor will brag about his freedom to you, his relief from anxiety, his independence. This is a dead beat, past resurrection, for everybody knows there ain't a more anxious dupe than he is. All his dreams are charcoal sketches of boarding-school misses. He dresses, greases his hair, paints his mustache, cultivates bunions and corns, to please his captains, the women, and only gets laughed at for his pains.

I tried being an old bachelor and had more sharp pains in one year than I have had since. I was in a lively fever all the time. There is only one person who has inhabited this world thus far that I think could have been a bachelor and done the subject justice and he was Adam. But since Adam saw fit to open the ball I hold it is every man's duty to select a partner and keep the dance hot.

But there were certain preliminaries that you have to go through with — ordinarily — before marriage. Josh loved all of these and particularly that of courting.

Courting is a hug-and-kiss match, generally a draw. The man who has never courted has lived in vain. He has been a blind man among landscapes and waterscapes. He has been a deaf man in the land of hand organs and by the side of murmuring streams.

Courting is like 2 little springs of soft water that steal out from under a rock at the foot of a mountain and run down the hill, side by side, singing and dancing and spattering each other, eddying and frothing and cascading, now hiding under the bank, now full of sun and now full of shadow, till by-and-by they join and then go slow.

Courting is like eating strawberries and cream — wants to be did slow, then you get the flavor.

In courting I have always advised the oblique; if your mistress discovers too much anxiety in you, she is sure to discover less in herself.

About the hardest work a fellow can do is to spark two gals at once and preserve a good average.

Young man, you can rely upon Josh Billings, and if you can't make these rules work just send for him and he will show you how the thing is did, and it shan't cost you a cent.

And furthermore, young man, what is courting without kissing?

The more a man undertakes to tell about a kiss the more he will reduce his ignorance to a science. You can't analyze a kiss any more than you can the breath of a flower. You can't tell what makes a kiss taste so good any more than you can a peach. Any man who can set down, where it is cool, and tell how a kiss tastes, ain't got any more real flavor to his mouth than a knothole has. The only way to describe a kiss is to take one, and then set down, all alone, out of the draft, and smack your lips. If you can't satisfy yourself how a kiss tastes without taking another one, how on earth can you define it to the next man?

I describe a kiss as the time and spot where affection comes to the surface.

I want it understood that I am talking about pure emotional kissing, that is born in the heart and flies to the lips, like a hummingbird to her roost. I am not talking about your lazy, milk-and-molasses kissing that daubs the face of anybody, nor your savage bite that goes around like a roaring lion in search of something to eat.

Kissing an unwilling pair of lips is as mean a victory as robbing a bird's nest and kissing too willing ones is about as unfragrant a recreation as making bouquets out of dandelions.

The kind of kissing that I am talking about is the kind that must do it — or spoil!

Kissing that husbands give and take is simply gathering ripe fruit from one's own plum tree that would otherwise drop off or be stolen.

I can't tell whether there is any particular etiquette to be observed in administering a kiss or not. Between lovers it is sometimes usual to kiss and hang on, but it strikes me that the best way is to come up front face, in single file, then fire and fall back one pace. This gives the patients a chance to get the flavor. The great beauty of a kiss lies in its impulsiveness and its impressibility — two pretty big words but worth the money.

I haven't done anything in the kissing line (of an amateur nature) of late years, and there may be some new dodge that I ain't posted in, but the old-fashioned 25-year-ago kind, I remember fresh. That kind didn't have any mathematics in it, but was more like spontaneous combustion.

It is hard work to be in love and not act foolish, but love is the only thing I know of that makes folly excusable. Love has made some kind of a fool of every man it has attacked since the days of Adam, and it made the biggest kind of a fool of him. Wisdom and ambition is no protection against the disease, for Solomon evaporated before it like the dew before the morning sun, and even good old David wilted like the hewn grass.

Love believes four times as much as it can prove and can prove four times as much as anyone else believes.

Trying to define love is like trying to tell you how you came to break through the ice — all you know about it is you fell in and got *ducked*. We speak of "falling in love" without thinking that it is the only way to get in love — we all stumble into it and can seldom tell *how* or *why*. The best cure for love is to live on it.

Love is said to be blind but I know lots of fellows in love who can see twice as much in their gals as I can.

There is in this life a vast deal of love that has no more virtue in it than wooden nutmegs have. There is "love undying" that generally lives about as long as uncorked ginger pop does. There is "love untold" which is always told to anybody who will listen to it and is as full of pathos as pork-and-beans is of nightmares. There is "love at sight" to which I will add "love for 90 days." And there is "love lies bleeding" — this is probably one of the bloodiest lies that ever was told.

If you want to cure love I have a few suggestions.

Put a plaster on your back, and see if that won't help you. If it don't get any better, wash in kerosene oil, and eat some green persimmons. If that don't make you feel any more easier, get seasick and lift up things. This will cure 9 times out of 10.

If you find you don't get any better, take another dose of seasickness. If you keep a-getting, finally, more worse, you have got the real old yellow love and no mistake.

There is only one cure for this kind, and that is the oil of wedlock. But this is very powerful, and wants to be took with great caution. I have known one dose of it to give a man fits for life.

It is hoped before you got this far you found the right kind of a girl.

Find a girl that is 19 years old last May, about the right height, with a blue eye, and dark brown hair and white teeth. Let the girl be good to look at, not too fond of music, a firm believer in ghosts, and one of six children in the same family. Look well to the character of her father; see that he is not the member of any club, don't bet on elections, and gets shaved at least three times a week.

Find out about her mother. See if she has got a heap of good common sense, study well her likes and dislikes, eat some of her homemade bread and apple dumplings, notice whether she abuses all of her neighbors, and don't fail to observe whether her dresses are last year's ones fixed over.

If you are satisfied that the mother would make the right kind of a mother-in-law you can safely conclude that the daughter would make the right kind of a wife.

After these preliminaries are all settled and you have done a reasonable amount of sparking, ask the young lady for her heart and hand, and if she refuses, you can consider yourself euchred. If on the contrary she should say yes, get married at once, without any fuss and feathers, and proceed to take the chance.

Marriage is a trap that men set themselves, then bait, and then deliberately get into, and then — GROWL!

Marriage is older than the pyramids and as full of hieroglyphics that nobody can parse. History holds its tongue who the pair was who first put on the silken harness and promised to work kind in it, through thick and thin, up hill and down, and on the level, rain or shine, survive or perish, drown or float.

But whoever they was they must have made a good thing out of it, or so many of their posterity would not have harnessed up since and drove out.

There is a great moral grip in marriage; it is the mortar that holds the social bricks together. But there ain't but darn few folks who could set down and give a good written opinion why on earth they come to do it.

Some marry for beauty, and never discover their mistake — this is lucky.

Some marry for money — and don't see it.

Some marry for pedigree and feel big for six months; then they come to the conclusion that pedigree ain't no better than skim milk.

Some marry to please their kinfolks and are surprised to learn that their kinfolks don't care a cuss for them afterwards.

Some marry for love without a cent in their pocket, nor a friend in the world, nor a drop of pedigree. This looks desperate, *but it is the strength of the game.*

Some marry because they think women will be scarce next year, and live to wonder how the crop holds out.

Some marry they don't know why and live they can't tell how.

Some marry in haste and then set down and think it carefully over.

Some think it carefully over first, and then set down and marry.

Some marry flirts. This is like buying a poor farm, heavily mortgaged, and working the balance of your days to clear off the mortgage.

Married life has its chances and this is just what gives it its flavor. Everybody loves to gamble because everybody expects to win. But I am authorized to state that everybody don't win.

Nobody can swear exactly where he will fetch up when he touches calico. No man can tell just what calico has made up its mind to do next. Calico don't know even herself.

If anybody asks you why you got married tell him you *don't recollect.*

Marriage is a safe way to gamble—if you win, you win a pile, and if you lose, you don't lose anything only the privilege of living dismally alone and soaking your own feet.

Don't marry a man to reform him; a man that can't reform himself is not worth reforming anyhow.

Marriage is an altar on which a man lays his pocketbook and a woman her love letters.

I had rather be married to an unabridged Webster's dictionary than to an unabridged literary woman.

Marrying for beauty is a poor speculation—for any man who sees your wife has got just about as much stock in her as you have.

Marrying a woman for her money is very much like setting a rattrap and baiting it with your own finger.

Married life is too often like a game of checkers—a struggle to get into the king row.

Cool weather is the best time to marry.

When you are married don't swap with your mother-in-law unless you can afford to give her the big end of the trade.

Not long after Henry got married he had other things to talk about which were close to his heart:

The first baby has become one of the fixed stars of life, and ever since the first one was born, on the wrong side of the Garden of Eden, down to the little stranger of yesterday, they have never failed to be a budget of much joy, an event of much gladness.

To wake up some cheerful morning and see a pair of soft eyes looking into yours—to wonder how so much beauty could have been entrusted to you—to search out the father, or the mother, in the sweet little face, and then lose the survey, in an instant of beauty as a laughing angel lays before you—to play with the golden hair and sow fond kisses upon this little bird in your nest—'tis this that makes the first baby the joy of all joys—a feast of the heart.

To find the pale mother again by your side, more lovely than when she was wooed — to see a new tenderness in her eye, and to hear the chastened sweetness of her laugh, as she tells something new about the baby — to love her far more than ever — and to find ofttimes a prayer on your lips — 'tis this that makes the first baby a fountain of sparkling pleasure.

To watch the bud of your rosebush — to catch the first notes of your songbird — to hear the warm praise of kind friends — and to give up your hours to the treasure — 'tis this that makes the first baby a gift that angels have brought you.

To look upon the track that life takes — to see the sunshine and shower — to plead for the best and shrink from the worst — to shudder when sickness steals on — and to be chastened when death comes — 'tis this — oh! 'tis this that makes the first baby a hope upon earth and a gem up in heaven.

If I could have my way, I would change all the human beings on the face of the earth back into babies at once and keep them there, and make this footstool one grand nursery. But what I would do for wet nurses I don't know nor don't care.

I would like to have 15 babies now on my lap and my lap ain't the handiest lap in the world for babies neither. My lap is long enough, but not the widest kind of lap. I am a good deal of a man, but I consist of length principally and when I make a lap of myself it is not a mattress but more like a couple of rails with a joint in them.

I can hold more babies in my lap at once than any man in America without spilling one — but it hurts the babies.

I never saw a baby in my life that I didn't want to kiss. I am worse than an old maid in this respect. I have seen babies that I have refused to kiss until they had been washed but the baby wasn't to blame for this — neither was I.

There are folks in this world who say they don't love babies but you can depend upon it when they was babies somebody loved them. Babies love me, too. I can take them out of their mother's arms just as easy as I can an unfledged bird out of his nest. They love me because I love them.

And here let me say, for the comfort and consolation of all mothers, that whenever they see me on the cars or on the steamboat, out of a job, they needn't hesitate a minute to drop a clean, fat baby onto my lap. I will hold it and kiss it and be thankful besides.

Perhaps there is people who don't envy me all this, but it is one of the sharp-cut, well-defined joys of my life, my love for babies and their love for me.

Perhaps there is people who will call it a weakness, but I don't care what they call it. Bring on the babies. Uncle Josh has always a kind word and a kiss for the babies.

I love babies for the truth there is in them. I ain't afraid their kiss will betray me. There is no frauds, dead beats nor counterfeits among them.

Babies I love with all my heart. They are my sweetmeat; they warm up my blood like a gin sling; they crawl into me and nestle by the side of my soul, like a kitten under a cookstove.

I have raised babies myself and know what I am talking about.

CHAPTER FOUR

"Josh Billings" Is Born

"Early genius, like early cabbage, don't head well."

In 1854 Shaw moved his family to Poughkeepsie, New York, and went into the real estate and auctioneering business. The latter was great training for his lecturing later on. However, it, like real estate, did not offer to his flowering genius an opportunity to "head well." He later wrote:

The auctioneer is an unfortunate individual who does other people's lying for 10 dollars a day and boards himself. He has got as much jaw as a wolf trap, and as much cheek as a 10-year-old mule. He takes up the profession quite often on the same principle that a horse doctor does — not because he is fit for the business, but just to have one in the neighborhood. His greatest pride is to mingle what he calls humor with his talk when he is on the block. But his jokes are generally as flat and as level as a cold flapjack. He is at the height of his ambition when he has worried a laugh out of the bystanders, and he uses the same rhetoric and similes when he sells out a line of bank securities that he does when he closes out an old one-eyed pelter under a chattel mortgage in front of the courthouse. A country auctioneer and a country horse trader are two wonderful cusses in the rural districts.

It must have been lots of fun to read advertisements for the sale of real estate such as this that Josh used:

To sell for eighteen hundred and thirty-nine dollars a palace, a sweet and pensive retirement located on the virgin banks of the Hudson containing 85 acres. The land is luxuriously divided by the hand of nature and art, into pasture and tillage, into plain and declivity, into stern abruptness, and the dalliance of moss-tufted meadow streams of sparkling gladness (thick with trout) dance through this wilderness of beauty, to the low music of the cricket and grasshopper.

It was fortunate that Henry was tied down by family and business. Neither one took up all of his boundless physical and imaginative mental energy. He began dabbling with little humorous sketches which he first sent to the New Ashford Eagle, *a newspaper in a small town north of Lanesboro. They were written in a form that had great vogue at the time — letters in a dialect purporting to report what was happening in a rural community. The letters of "Major Jack Downing" had made this form of humorous writing almost a national pastime. Shaw signed them as "Efren Billings." Here is a selection from one of them, translated out of its almost unreadable dialect:*

The kind of dancing I practiced in my younger days was to a fiddle and the drumming of cowhide boots to regulate the time. Twenty years ago there wasn't ten men in Ashford that could beat me for heel and toe in an old-fashioned breakdown and jig. The gals allow that I was equal to all nature at a double shuffle or a pigeon wing, and when I done the Fisher's Hornpipe to the tune of "My Wife's Dead, and I'm a Widower,"

I'm going down to Roasarins river,
High heel boots and cotton stockings
Come dance to me, Miss Polly Hopkins,

the audience not infrequently rose from their seats and called for three cheers.

As to dancing now, it's not on the cards; my will is good but one of my legs was took with the rheumatiz last fall and since then there has been no regular spring to it. It's an awful nuisance for the other one is as pert as ever, and to have a two-forty leg on one side, and a spavin consarn that goes with a drag and a jerk on the other, is worse than ridiculous.

A mixture of mustard, oil and vitriol, red pepper, and chloroform, has been recommended to me as a good liniment in such cases, but I haven't tried it yet.

Friends in Poughkeepsie talked Shaw into writing for the local papers. He did so under the pseudonym of "Sledlength" on the condition that he would not write in dialect. A number of his pieces appeared in the Poughkeepsian *and the* Poughkeepsie Daily Press. *But they attracted no attention outside of the city itself.*

The way for a writer to build a reputation then was for other newspapers to reprint his writings. One of Shaw's sketches had been "An Essay on the Mule." After this had appeared, and had not been picked up by other newspapers, he read a somewhat similar piece by Artemus Ward that had been reprinted all over the country. The difference was that Ward's piece had been in dialect. As an experiment Shaw translated his piece on the mule into dialect and sent it to a Boston newspaper. A short while later he received an acceptance notice — and a check for $1.50. His first impulse was to send the check back — with a note of condolence to the publisher that such generosity might bankrupt him. But he didn't. "I think I have touched oil," he said. And he had. The piece was reprinted all over the country and gave him almost instant fame. From then on everything that he wrote was under the name Josh Billings.

From now on Shaw insisted on payment for everything that he did. This got him many rejections, at first, but in the long run gave him a reputation as a professional.

In the Civil War, Shaw wrote no "flag-waving" propaganda; he made no effort to join the army — he did not have to, having a wife and two daughters and being in his middle forties. Yet there is little doubt that his humor was a great morale builder in this time of stress and strain, and his sketches were avidly read by President Lincoln.

Josh did one little sketch which gives his viewpoint on the war:

I am a black Republican, with white antecedents.

I always was against slavery of any kind; not because it was unconstitutional, but because it was ungodly.

I don't believe the best judges of color can pick out a Negro's soul in the Kingdom of Heaven.

Josh also gave some war definitions which must have made Lincoln bellylaugh:

A Successful Raid — cutting off a turnpike within the enemy's lines, and bringing in a blind mule, and 2 Negroes to board.

Base of Supplies — Uncle Sam's pocketbook.

Military Necessity — Ten officers and a gallon of whiskey to every three privates.

War of Extermination — this phase belongs wholly to the Commissary Department.

Military Strategy — trying to reduce a swamp by catching the bilious fever in it.

Later, after Lincoln's assassination, during blind-hatred Reconstruction, Josh gave his opinion of Thaddeus Stevens by telling an anecdote:

Give me leave to recite a little dream I had last night. I fancied I was in hell and while engaged in conversation with the proprietor, an imp announced that Mr. Stevens was at the door desiring admittance. Old Nick promptly refused his entrance because Stevens would be continually disturbing the peace and order of the place. The imp soon returned, saying that Thaddeus insisted on coming in, declaring that he had no other place to go to. After some deliberation Old Nick's face brightened with a new idea and he exclaimed:

"I've got it. Tell the janitor to give him six bushels of brimstone and a box of matches, and let him go and start a little place of his own."

Abe Lincoln would have loved — and understood — that one.

On a drizzly October day in 1863 another phase of Josh's career began. The pastor of the Congregational church at Poughkeepsie, Reverend Leonard Corning, with a friend, George W. Sterling, came to Josh's office and asked him to deliver a lecture composed of his writings.

"In a life of foolhardly things," Josh answered, "this would be the most foolhardy."

But the two friends would not take no for an answer. They made him sit down and give them a preview, from his sketches, of what he would say. And he kept them roaring with laughter for two hours.

When it was announced that Josh was going to give the lecture, it was said that "a broad grin stretched clear across town." Every man, woman and child in the place knew him and loved him.

The evening came, the hall was packed, and when Josh strode out before them, without introduction — as he always insisted upon — his six-foot, two-hundred-pound body slouched forward, his face as solemn as an owl's, a roar of laughter greeted him. And that roar shuttled between tears and crescendos for two hours. Equally as important, the audience had paid two hundred dollars into the till for the privilege of hearing him.

This proved to be one of those things that are blown up too fast. Josh hired a manager and set off on a lecture tour. Close to home, where his sketches had given him a solid reputation, he had good turnouts. But as he went westward, the people started staying away in droves. Finally that specter that haunts all speakers became a reality — only one man turned up for the lecture.

"Will the audience move a little closer and occupy the front seat?" Josh said. The man complied. "Now would the audience like to go around the corner with the lecturer and have some fried oysters?"

The "audience" would, and they had a most pleasant evening.

At Milwaukee, Wisconsin, no one turned up for the lecture. Josh checked with his manager and found that they had enough money to get back to Poughkeepsie on. He then called his landlord to his room, and asked him to have some wine with them.

"I have tied strings around my lecture," he said, "and I'm going to lay it gently on a good bed of coals and see it go up in smoke."

The landlord, who had read many of Josh's sketches and loved them, protested. Finally, after they were mellowed by several bottles of wine, Josh agreed to give it another trial.

Back in Poughkeepsie, Josh worked furiously to get together enough material for a book. He had to make up — both for his pride and his finances — for his flop as a lecturer. But after it was finished, he didn't know what to do with it. On a gamble he wrote Artemus Ward telling him about the manuscript and asking his advice. Artemus immediately invited Josh down to New York for a talk — and Josh was on the next train that ran. When he reached Artemus's hotel, at about three o'clock in the afternoon, he found a gay crowd having "supper" which consisted of liquids only. Among those present were Henry Clapp, editor of *Vanity Fair*, Martin M. Thompson, the creator of Doesticks, Robert Newell, whose pseudonym was Orpheus C. Kerr — a take-off on "office seekers" — and of course Artemus himself. Josh, as well he could, joined in the festivities. That evening he heard Artemus "speak a piece" at a lecture hall.

After the lecture Artemus took Josh back to his room where he read the manuscript, stopping often to slap his leg and roar with laughter. The next day he took Josh to meet his publisher, G. W. Carleton, who, after reading the manuscript, agreed to publish the book. It came out in 1865 as *Josh Billings, His Sayings*.

In May, 1866, Josh began writing a column for Smith & Street's *New York Weekly*, the *Saturday Evening Post* of the period, and continued to write it until his death. In the 1870's he also began writing a column for the *Century Magazine* not in dialect and under the pseudonym of Uncle Ezek. "There ain't no more wit and wisdom in *bad spelling than there is in being cross-eyed," he wrote. "You can't make a weak sentence strong by spelling it right, nor a strong sentence weak by spelling it wrong." Josh was a good enough showman and psychologist to give the people what they wanted — not what he thought they ought to have.*

When Josh's book got good reviews in the London Athenaeum, *the London* Queen, The London Spectator, *and in various French publications like the* Revue des Deux Mondes, *Josh began sending copies to cities that had not supported his lectures, or had turned him down, with a note like this:*

I have sent you by today's mail a copy of the London Spectator containing an extended criticism of "Josh Billings," and as you will observe of the most flattering character. I have done this, not expecting that you will alter your opinion in reference to him, but to show you what consummate asses those English papers are making of themselves.

This fetched them! Before long Josh was getting more invitations to make lectures than he could fill. Unlike Mark Twain and Artemus Ward — and like Will Rogers — Josh loved to travel and to talk to and meet people. He did not mind the uncomfortable beds, the bad food, the dirt and the inconvenience — although he did not like the bedbugs. He simply took these things as part of the game. They all vanished in the joy of being out with "the real bird" and picking up what he had to say, and studying what he was thinking, at the source, then translating it back in a way that he would remember.

What Josh wrote about comic lecturing is probably the best description of its pitfalls and possibilities that has been written:

Comic lecturing is an uncommon pesky thing to do. It is more uncertain than the rat-catching business as a means of grace, or as a means of livelihood.

Most anybody thinks he can do it, and this is just what makes it so bothersome to do. When it is did just enough, it is a terrific success, but when it is overdid, it is like a burnt slapjack, very impertinent.

There ain't but few good judges of humor, and they all differ about it.

If a lecturer tries to be funny, he is like a horse trying to trot backwards, pretty apt to trod on himself.

Humor must fall out of a man's mouth like music out of a bobolink, or a young bird out of its nest when it is feathered enough to fly.

Whenever a man has made up his mind that he is a wit, then he is mistaken without remedy, but whenever the public has made up their mind that he has got the disease, then he has got it sure.

Individuals never get this thing right, the public never gets it wrong.

Humor is wit with a rooster's tail feather stuck in its cap, and wit is wisdom in tight harness.

If a man is a genuine humorist, he is superior to the

bulk of his audience, and will often have to take his pay for his services in thinking so.

Although fun is designed for the millions, and ethics for the few, it is as true as molasses, that most all audiences have their bellwethers, people who show the others the crack where the joke comes laughing in. I have known popular audiences deprived of all pleasure during the recital of a comic lecture, just because the right man, or the right woman, wasn't there to point out the mellow places.

The man who is anxious to get before an audience with what he calls a comic lecture ought to be put immediately in the stocks so that he can't do it, for he is a dangerous person to get loose, and will do some damage.

It is a very pleasant business to make people laugh, but there is much odds whether they laugh *at you,* or laugh *at what you say.*

When a man laughs *at you,* he does it because it makes him feel superior to you, but when you please him with what you have uttered, he admits that you are superior to him.

The only reason why a monkey always creates a sensation wherever he goes, is simply because—he is a monkey.

Everybody feels as though they had a right to criticize a comic lecture, and most of them do it just as a mule criticizes things, by shutting up both eyes and letting drive with his two behind legs.

One of the meanest things in the comic lecturing employment that a man has to do is to try to make that large class of his audience laugh whom the Lord never intended should laugh.

There is some who laugh as easy and as natural as the birds sing, but most of mankind laughs like a hand organ — if you expect to get a lively tune out of it you have got to grind for it.

For twenty seasons beginning in 1865 Josh "read" his lectures in every city in the country over 20,000 and in hundreds that did not have many more than a thousand.

His friend, and biographer, Francis M. Smith, tells an interesting experience that Josh had in California on a lecture tour. While passing over the mountains to fill an engagement at Grass Valley and Placerville, Josh rode outside of the coach with the driver. As the stage stopped at a watering place for the horses, the driver told him to go inside a shanty that stood near and see what he would find there. Josh pushed the door open and entered. A man of about sixty was frying bacon in a long-handled spider over a wood fire.

"My friend," Josh said, "I have come two thousand miles out of my way to see you."

"Is that so, stranger? What will you take to drink?"

Josh joined the old man in a glass of villainous whiskey. Then he bade him good-by — feeling that he should talk to him more — and joined the driver on the outside of the stage.

"How did you like him?" asked the driver.

"He looks like a prospector who has panned out," Josh said.

"He's James Marshall," the driver said, "who picked up the first piece of gold found in California. The state pays him an annuity of one hundred and fifty dollars a month."

Josh published another book, *Josh Billings on Ice*, in 1868 before he stumbled onto the phase of writing which gave him his greatest fame.

In March, 1869, Josh was laid up with a cold at Skowhegan, Maine, and while remaining in his hotel room read an issue of the *Old Farmer's Almanac.* He decided that a comic take-off on this solid sinew of New England would sell. He accordingly made up a sample and sent it to G. W. Carleton, offering to sell it to him for $250 and to do one like it each year for ten years. Carleton liked the idea but told Josh that he would be crazy to sell the idea outright and offered instead to publish it on a royalty basis. The first issue of *Josh Billings' Farmer's Allminax for 1870* sold over 90,000 copies and thereafter for the remaining nine years over 127,000 copies a year. Instead of getting $2500 Josh got well over $30,000 for this item.

Josh did his best writing for the *Allminax.* A compilation of them, *Old Probability, Perhaps Rain, Perhaps Not,* 1879, was his favorite book.

With money flowing in from a number of sources, Josh moved his family to New York and gave them the luxuries that heretofore he hadn't been able to afford. Always a great lover of horses himself, he got for Zilpha a pair of "electric spinners" and a handsome brougham, and almost *any fine day she could be seen with the girls, and later with the grandchildren, in Central Park, driven by a nobby coachman.*

Josh loved New York. When there, between lecture and vacation trips, it was his custom to walk the three miles from his apartment on Central Park to the office of the New York Weekly *where he had a desk. After an hour or so there, spent either in writing or in talking, he would saunter through town on Broadway to the Fifth Avenue Hotel under which G. W. Carleton had his office. Josh had another desk there where he received his official mail. After answering this he went home, usually in time for lunch, and spent the afternoon writing.*

When summer came Josh packed up his family, hitched up a surrey, and headed for the trout streams of the White Mountains. They went by slow stages, enjoying themselves on the way, and Josh never passed up a likely-looking spot where trout might lurk.

Francis M. Smith went with him one summer. No matter what happened Josh caught trout. Smith couldn't get one to rise. Finally, in fishing one stream, they came to a beautiful hole.

"There, Frank," Josh said, "there are beauties in that hole. I'll go on up the stream and come back later."

When Josh got back, with his creel full, Smith still hadn't caught a thing.

"I tell you," Josh insisted, "there are trout in there — just look."

He flicked his fly and it hardly touched the water, as

gentle as thistledown, when it was seized by a three-quarter-pound speckled beauty. Josh kept on until he had landed four in a few moments.

In the Allminax *for 1870, on the date page for June, Josh has this little doggerel:*

> Now bait your hook and find a brook,
> Where water runs the fastest;
> There lays the trout, just jerk him out,
> And chuck him in your basket.

But it was up to New Ashford, near where he was born, that Josh liked to go when he took a real vacation. He tells about it in a way that would make "back-to-nature" enthusiasts out of most people if there was any such "nature" still there for the taking:

The village of New Ashford is located in Massachusetts about 150 miles west of Plymouth Rock. If you love a mountain come up here and see me. Right in front of the little tavern where I am staying rises up a chunk of land that will make you feel weak to look at it. I have been on its top, and far above was the bright blue sky, without a cloud swimming in it, while below me the rain shot slanting on the valley and the lightning played its mad pranks.

How still this New Ashford is. At sunrise the roosters crow all around, once apiece; at sunset the cows come hollering home to be milked; and at twilight out steal the crickets with a song the burden of which seems sad and weary. This is all the racket there is in New Ashford. It is so still here that you can hear a feather drop from a bluejay's tail.

Out of this mountain, squeezed by the weight of it, leaks a little brook of water, and up and down this brook each day I loiter. In my hand I have a short pole, on the end of the pole a short line, and on the line a sharp hook, and looped on the hook a grub, or worm.

Every now and then there comes dancing out of this little brook a live trout no longer than your finger, but as sweet as a stick of candy, and in he goes at the top of my basket. This is what I am here for: trout for breakfast, trout for dinner, and trout for supper.

I am as happy and as lazy as a yearling heifer. I have not a care on my mind, not an ache in my body. I haven't read a newspaper for a week, and wouldn't read one for a dollar.

I shall stay here till my money gives out and shall come back to the senseless crash of the city with a tear in my eye and holes in both of my boots.

The world is full of fun but most folks look too high for it.

I am coming home, dear friends, in two months, and then I will set down in your little sanctum and whisper to you. It is so still here that a whisper sounds loud; a still noise is another name, I believe, for happiness.

The first thing I do in the morning, when I get up, is to go out and look at the mountain, and see if it is there. If this mountain should go away, how lonesome I should be. Yesterday, I picked one quart of field strawberries, caught

27 trout, and gathered a whole parcel of wintergreen leaves — a big day's work. When I got home last night tired, no man could have bought them of me for 700 dollars, but I suppose, after all, that it was the *tired* that was worth the money. There is a great deal of raw bliss in getting tired.

It is now 9 o'clock P.M. and every thing in New Ashford is fast asleep including the crickets. I will just step out and see if the mountain is there, and then I will go to bed.

Oh! The bliss of living up in New Ashford, close by the side of a great giant mountain to guard you, where everything is as still as a boy's tin whistle at midnight. A mosquito couldn't live long enough to take one bite where board is 4 dollars a week and everybody, cats and all, at 9 o'clock P.M. are fast asleep and snoring.

Trout fishing is a good deal like painting pictures — you are born knowing how; you can't learn how. It don't require the genius of a statesman to know how to catch a trout; but the two best trout fishers I ever knew was Daniel Webster and old Ishmael. Both were natives of New England; one of them everybody is proud to remember, and the other was a simple old Negro; but I think the old darky was the best fisher of the two.

He would walk up to a hole in the brook, where a big trout lay as careless and yet as still as a hen turkey, and stand there till the fish mistook him for the stub of a tree, then would drop his worm, or his grasshopper, or (if the season was right) would dance his flies above the trout's head so literal that the fish would bite merely from the force of habit, whether he was hungry or not.

This old Negro always started out for trout just as a dog does for mischief, the other way from where he was going, and never come back without a trophy.

Go with me sometime next May among the mountains and I will show you how to win these little spotted morsels from their wet and noisy homes. But — though I like company generally — to be honest about it, trout fishing is a good deal like sparking — one feller at a time is enough.

In answer to queries sent in to him at the Allminax, *Josh gave out certain bits of interesting information:*

Have you ever been to Pordunk, my native village?

It is a dear little lullaby of a place sleeping between two small mountains. It contains about 1000 souls now, and is watered by Goose Creek which meanders through the village as crooked as a schoolboy on his way to the district schoolhouse.

I was born there, and the ground on which the old house stood is there yet. My ancestors are all here, too, but they have retired from business, and are taking their ease in the old graveyard of the little one-story church.

The Billings have been a healthy old breed as far back as I have dug for them, which they owe principally to a milk diet. It is said that Behomath Billings, one of our pristines, could drain a cow perfectly dry at one sitting.

If this is so, it helps explain the great amount of milk in the Billings' nature.

I don't find any old bachelors, nor old maids, among our ancestors; increase and multiply has always been the battle cry of the Billings.

Adam Billings was the first of the Billingses. He was named after the first man and it was said by his friends he resembled his illustrious namesake in form and features. His temper was as even as the figure 2 and his habits as pure as the mountain dew. He went barefooted until his 32nd year, and is said to have been one of the best dancers in the entire neighborhood.

He was very fond of the marvelous, indeed I have always thought his great-great-grandson, your Uncle Josh, inherited this particular trait from him in a very marked degree. I really don't believe the old man intended to lie; but to put it mildly, he did at times handle the truth in a very careless and reckless manner.

Zephaniah Billings was a fiddler by birth and persuasion. He also had another natural gift, and that was to owe everybody.

He would travel on foot 7 miles to a country tavern and fiddle all night at a country ball for 75 cents, and owe the landlord two dollars and a half next morning for vittles and drink.

Late in life he quit fiddling and took up shoemaking; but the world lost a good fiddler and got a cussed poor shoemaker.

Zeph died finally, and I presume he was saved; but he

may have been lost, for accidents will happen in the uppermost families.

Jehosophat Billings was never known to waste anything by giving it away. The great extravagance of his life, and the one he never forgot to speak of, was giving 3 dollars towards building the Pordunk meetinghouse. After he give the money, he took such a deep interest in the work on the meetinghouse that the committee was obliged to give him back the money to get shut of him. He swore he'd sue them for the interest on the money, but he never did.

Jehoss died at the age of 63, if I have searched right, from an overdose of clam chowder drank at a free lunch. What has become of him I can't state. I would like to say some more about Jehoss, but I can't without telling the truth. Truth is sometimes like a hot potato, the only way to handle it easy is to drop it.

Melkisidek Billings was a dandy of the old school, and also a great lover. He loved the whole entire female population. He parted his hair in the middle, and did it uncommon even. He was a punctilious man, in his everyday wear, and dressed chuck up to the fashion. He didn't have much brains, but he didn't need much, for his business through life was the lover business.

Just before he died he married and left one daughter, a sentimental offspring, who afterwards run away, at the age of 16, with a dancing master.

Solomon Billings was known far and near for his chunks of wisdom but, like Solomon of old, he could talk wisdom better than he could do it. This is the way with all the wise men I have met lately.

Solomon could tell, by looking at the egg, how much a gosling would weigh before it was born, and when the best time was to set a hen or a gatepost.

Sol's mouth was full of wisdom. Lightning couldn't strike a tree just for fun but he would preach a moral sermon from the text. He was dreadful certain of what he did know and wasn't the least bit uncertain of what he didn't know.

I find in digging down to the hard pan of Solomon, my ancestor, that he had a great deal of vanity, a large amount of impudence, a good supply of incredulity — just the things for all the world to make a wise fool out of.

Deuteronomy Billings was the same kind of a man in the fall as he was in the spring of the year; you didn't have to winter him to find out who he was. He always did as he agreed, but was dreadful backward about agreeing.

Deuteronomy was immense in one thing, and that was the length of his nose. He had more nose than any man in history. One writer says his nose was 8 inches in length and another makes it a fraction over 10 inches. I will split the difference and call it 7. If Dute was alive I think he would sustain my figgers.

Porkanbeans Billings could swap a horse closer than any man that impartial history tells of. He is said to have swapped Deacon Absolem Featherweight clean out of a 5-year-old sorrel horse, at one swap, and the deacon was looked upon as almost insurmountable in a dicker.

Porky was a horse trader of the ancient days, one who hung around the village tavern, and always had on hand an old flag-tailed pelter, with a glass eye, to trade with anybody.

I don't feel like bragging of Porkanbeans as an ancestor, but I must say, as a horse trader (if all reports are true) I feel proud of him. I forgot to state that Porky left no property. There is a great deal of genius in the horse-swap business but few assets.

Porkanbeans died instantly, somewhere about the first of the 17th century. He was struck by the hind feet of a mule. Moral character even won't save a fellow being from dissolution when a mule goes for him with both hind feet at once.

Jamaica Billings was said by good judges of the article to be the laziest man that ever visited this world. At the age of 14 he was pronounced by the doctors too lazy to catch flies. He was named after his uncle who had a great specialty in the Jamaica rum line, and who could float more ardent spirits, on an evener keel, than any human craft in those days.

Jamaica was born tired and never outgrew it. He married at 37 but his wife left him at the end of the first month of their nuptials, taking with her all personal effects, which were a couple of cedar washtubs and a secondhand buggy harness, brass-mounted. Her first name was Polly Ann. They never met afterwards.

Jamaica spent his life in hanging around places, keeping ragged and fat on nothing. He kind of lazied to death, and I suppose was buried, but history don't say so, in just so many words.

Ecclesiastes Billings was a Puritan by nature and occupation. He was as Puritan as spring lamb soaked in mint sauce. Some of the most cold and thawless stock in all New England oozed from Ecclesiastes Billings. He had his trunk packed to come over in the Mayflower, but didn't come. He come over the next fall and went immediately into the Pilgrim business.

Ecclesiastes kept a grocery store, and never sanded his sugar, nor watered his New England rum without first asking to be forgiven for it.

Ecclesiastes was very tall, but then he was very thin; he was over 6 feet perpendicular, and not quite 7 inches through. He weighed 146 with his winter clothes and cowhide boots on. He preserved his thinity unto death. He died from eating too much garden truck.

Luke Billings was a schoolmaster of the New England type and shadow. He was an upright and an austere man, as upright as a sperm candle, and as austere as horse-radish.

I looked back onto Luke's memoirs and pity him, for I pity all district schoolmasters, all mothers-in-law, and all grass widows.

Luke Billings spent his whole life in the district school speculation, and died as poor as a salt codfish. His assets consisted of a pocket comb and a New Testament. He used to board round the neighborhood and was always as hungry as a pickerel.

Luke never got married; he hadn't the time to spare. He was engaged, for 26 years, to Nancy Burbanks, but they both died intestate. They sleep close together, in the old graveyard, at lower Pordunk.

Luke wore his hair long behind, and kept a district school 34 years 6 months and 17 days. He is an ancestor that I look back upon every now and then with my memory, and want to fight somebody on his account.

Nebecunezzar Billings was an orphan by birth, and kept a hotel. When you got fried pork at his house, it was fried pork. You didn't have a bill of fare to tell what it was.

His wife was smarter than chain lightning and cleaner than a ghost. Her hash didn't have any paving stones, nor cart wheels in it. You might as well hunt for the lost tribes of Israel on her premises as to hunt for a cockroach. She had red hair and was bony put together and could fry pork, tend bar, harness a horse, trade with a peddler, and make a gin sling that could almost talk.

Nebecunezzar was a politicianer and run hard for constable in old Pordunk many times. It is justice to his memoirs to state that though he run well, the office always beat him. He never got elected.

Neb spent his whole life in the hash business. His wife was boss while here on earth, and will undertake to be hereafter. But she can't, can she? Happy it is that there is a thusness in these things. Thrice happy.

In taking a square look back upon my ancestors, I find that their ambition was the result of vanity; their honesty the effect of education; their charity the love of novelty; their virtues more the growth of their pride than their humility; and their philosophy — able to bear the stomach-ache of others with heroic fortitude, but not worth a cuss in their own.

Eventually, of course, Josh got around to giving information about himself:

I am not a director in any horse railroad or baseball club.

I don't own stock in any rat pit.

I don't smoke but 3 cigars a day, and those, invariably good ones, at somebody else's expense.

I have been successfully married for over 30 years.

I never studied for the regular ministry.

I don't possess any horse and buggy.

I weigh 190 pounds — when I don't weigh more. I have two daughters and they are both united to men that suit me. I have no mother-in-law now extant. I don't keep any dog. I believe in a future state and its profits and losses. I am not a Freemason, nor don't travel with torchlight processions. I am very modest, but love apple dumplings to death — I am close on to 60 years old and was once a farmer, and a dreadful poor one too — I never had the dyspepsy nor fidgets but once, and ain't got rid of them yet — I sprung from New England — I write for fun and ducats combined — I have had some light touches of the rheumatiz, and never run for office that I didn't get beat

—I am temperance to a fault, never drinking milk until it has been thoroughly skimmed—I ain't got no politics, nor have as much religion as I ought to have—I have been all of my life looking for a ghost, and a honest man, and ain't seen one yet.

My age is a profound secret, but I was born in the old-fashioned way in the old of the moon; am long but crooked; don't believe in spirits (not even Jamaica spirits) and have never raised any boys to my knowledge on account of their liability to get out of repair.

My hair is black and quite tall behind. I wear a mustache and number 10 pegged boots. I have a sanguinary temperament and a bilious nose, eat as other folks do, except roasted goose. I can eat two of them and then a little more of that goose.

I work for my bread and roast goose, have a gray eye and am always ready to wag as the next dog.

I forgot to state that I was brought up by a Presbyterian church in Massachusetts, and am a good job.

When I was 20 I knew twice as much as I do now, and the ways things are going on, if I should live to be 75, I don't expect to know nothing.

If I should be called upon tomorrow to sign a receipt for this life, I feel that I can say I have never written a line in malice and that the world, as cold as many say they have found it, has treated me as well as I deserve.

I have studied my own character and my own impulses for 39 years closely, and I can't tell today (to save a bet) whether I am an honest and true man or not.

Q: Would you like to live your life over again?

A: Yes, if I could commence where I am now, and live it backwards and at the last be a boy again.

I know nothing about music. I don't know this tune from the other. I don't know "Yankee Doodle" from "Now I Lay Me Down on the Grass" or "Mary had an Infant Sheep."

I am uncommon sorry for this, but don't think that I am to blame for it. I have melody in me somewhere, for anybody can make me cry if they are careful. I love the tender as I do a rare boiled egg. I have shed many a tear, without anybody knowing it, over some mother's simple lullaby. But this is called mere weakness by the artists.

I am so fully aware of the uncertainty of the law that if a man whom I had never seen nor heard of should sue me for a *debt* of $100, and I couldn't compound with him for $50, I would pay the whole rather than defend the suit.

The first 3 notes I endorsed I had to pay, and I hope it will be just so with the next 3.

It is now 30 years since a fellow with green goggles on and a white necktie offered to sell me something for 50 cents which he said was worth 5 dollars. I've forgot what it was but I remember it was a beat and as often as once a year ever since I have tried the same thing over, and got beat every time. That's what you call a horn of dilemma.

"Horns of Dilemma" means a tight spot and has a horn at each end of it. There is no choice in these two horns.

If you seize one the other may perforate you and if you don't take either both of them may pitch into you.

I always avoid them if possible, but when possibility gives out, my rule is to shut up both eyes and fight both prongs with my whole grit. Nine times out of ten this will smash a dilemma and it is always a good fight if you get licked the tenth.

You can't argue or reason with the "horn of dilemma"; the only way is to advance in and fight for the gross amount.

I once took a farm on shares and run her on some theories and the thing figured up this way: I done all the work, furnished all the seed and manure, had the ague 9 months out of 12, for my share of the profits, and the other fellow paid the taxes on the farm for his share. By mutual consent I quit the farm at the end of the year.

The fact of it is that theories of all kind work well except in practice. They are too often designed to do the work of practice.

There ain't no theory in breaking a mule only to go at him with a club in your hand and some blood in your eye and break him just like you would a split log.

I undertook to break a kicking heifer once. I read a treatise on the subject and followed the directions close and got knocked endwise in about 5 minutes. I then sot down and thought the thing over. I made up my mind that the fellow who wrote the treatise was more in the treatise business than he was in the kicking-heifer trade.

I come to the conclusion that what he knew about milking kicking heifers he had learned by leaning over a barnyard fence and writing the thing up.

I got up from my reflections strengthened and went for that heifer. I will draw a veil over the language I used and the thing I did but I went in to win *and won.* That heifer never became a cow. There is one way to break a kicking heifer and that is that a kicking heifer is worth more for beef than she is for theoretic milk.

CHAPTER FIVE

Uncle Josh on Horses and Horse Racing

"Write me down as one who fears God and loves to catch trout, play whist and ride a 3-minute gait."

Josh loved fast, pretty horses. He also loved to horse trade. "I like a fast horse," he said, "and one that goes fast because he loves to. Such a critter is half human; he ought never to be hitched to a plow; he ought to be took out of his stable as a wild pigeon out of his cage and let — GO!"

Josh tells how to pick such a horse:

First — Let the color be a sorrel, a roan, a red, a gray, a white, a black, a blue, a green, a chestnut, a brown, a dapple, a spotted, a cream, a buckskin, or some other good color.

Second — Examine his ears; see that he has got two ears; pound a tin pan close to him to find out whether his hearing is good. All horses are dumb, but a deaf and dumb horse is not desirable.

Third — Look well to his eyes; see that he has got a pupil in his eyes and not too large a one either; horses with too large pupils in their eyes are nearsighted and can't see oats; and have to wear green goggles, and green goggles make a horse look too much like a tract peddler.

Fourth — Feel of his neck with the inside of your right hand; see that the spinal column is well fatted and runs the whole length of him from fore to aft; a horse without a good fat spinal column from fore to aft ain't worth (speaking sudden) a well-defined cuss.

Five — Put your hand on his breast (this is allowable in the case of quadrupeds) and see if his heart can beat 70; squeeze his forelegs to see if he is well muscled; lift up his before feet and see if there is any frogs in them; frogs keep a horse's feet cool and sweet, just as they do a well or a spring of water.

Six — Look well to his shoes, see what number he wears; number 8 is about right.

Seven — Run your hand along the dividing ridge of his body, from the top of his withers to the commencement of his tail and pinch him as you go along to see if he knows how to kick.

Eight — Look on his hind legs for some spavins, curbs, windgalls, ringbones, scratches, quittors, thrush, grease-heels, thoroughpins, springhalt, quarter cracks; see if he has got a whirlbone; look for some pin hips; hunt for strains in the back tendons, let-down and capped hocks.

Nine — Investigate his teeth, see if he ain't 14 years old last May, with teeth filed down, and a six-year-old black mark burnt into the top of them with a hot iron.

Ten — Smell of his breath to see if he ain't got some glanders; look just back of his ears for signs of pole evil;

pinch him on the top of his withers for fistula; and look sharp at both shoulders for a sweeny.

Eleven — Hook him to a wagon that rattles; drive him up to an Irishman and his wheelbarrow; meet a rag merchant with cowbells strung across the top of his cart; let a train pass him at 45 miles an hour; when he is sweaty leave a buffalo robe over him to keep off the cold; ride him with an umbrella histed; and learn his opinion of these things.

Twelve — Prospect his wind; search diligently for the heaves; ask if he is a roarer; and don't be afraid to find out if he is a whistler.

Thirteen — Be sure that he ain't a crib-biter; ain't balky; ain't a weaver; and don't pull at the halter.

These are a few simple things to be looked at in buying a *good family horse.* There is a great many other things to be looked at (at your leisure) after you have bought him.

Ask a man all about his wife and he may tell you, examine him close for a Sunday School teacher and find him all on the square, send him to the New York legislature and rejoice that money won't buy him, lend him seven hundred dollars in the highway without witness or note, even swap dogs with him with perfect impunity, and when you buy *a good family horse,* young, sound and true, watch the man close and make up your mind besides that you will have to ask the Lord to forgive him.

"An honest man is the noblest work of God," this famous saying was written in great anguish of heart by the late Alexander Pope just after buying *a good family horse.*

For a red-hot specialty, you have got to hunt creation close to find an equal to the country horse trader. He is always a man of pleasant temperament, vain of his opinions, often of more fancy than judgment, and quick to decide. He has but little real affection for a horse, and only loves him for the cheat that is in him. He is always ready to trade for anything, from a yearling colt to the cavalry horse Gen. Butler rode at the battle of Brandywine. He never knows when he gets cheated, and ever thinks that the last nag he got is the best one he ever owned. He is not bothered with too much conscience, and would as soon lay out a traveling preacher in a swap as his own father-in-law, and do it without any malice, but just for the honor of the profession.

I don't know why it is that a man can trade cows and be pious, or swap oxen, and be a good deacon, or even negotiate dogs, and be looked upon favorably, but when he goes into horse trading enterprise, if he can't cheat, he has mistaken his calling and ain't happy.

The horse trader is sometimes honest from policy, and the man who is simply honest from policy needs as much watching as a hive of bees do who are just getting ready to swarm.

Never swap horses with a deacon — not if you belong to the same church he does.

If you have got a horse that you ask 200 dollars for, and are offered 75 dollars for him, always sell him — don't spoil a good horse trade for $125.

If you should, by accident, get hold of a sound horse,

get shut of him as soon as you can, for you won't be happy with him.

If, in swapping horses, you get cornered, and can't lie, postpone the trade until next day.

Nobody ever expects to buy a horse without getting cheated; therefore, if a horse jockey don't lie, he loses one of his blessed privileges.

To swap a horse and not get beat,
Is something nice to brag on;
I tried it once, and that's the time
I lost a horse — and wagon.

Quite naturally Josh loved horse racing. He describes one that he attended:

"Great Race! at Sulphur Flat trotting Park, On Thursday, April 9th for a purse of 13 dollars and a bull's-eye watch. Free for all! Horses, Mares, Geldings, Mules and Jackasses!"

Seeing the above announcement pasted up on a guide-board at Jamaica Rum Four Corners, and having never seen a horse trot, on a well-regulated race course, *for the improvement of the breed of horses,* I agreed I would go, just to *encourage* the breeding of good horses.

I found the village of Sulphur Flats located in a lot and well watered by a gristmill and 2 tanneries.

The principal buildings seem to consist of a tavern, 3 groceries, an insurance office and another tavern — all conducted on strict whiskey principles.

I found the inhabitants a good deal tired in their religious views, and I thought the opening would admit 3 or 4 missionaries abreast.

The most principal business of the people was peeling bark in the winter, and pitching cents as soon as warm weather sot in.

I asked a gentleman, who said he was a reporter for the *Young Men's Christian Guide*, if he knew what the population of the place definitely was. He said he definitely didn't, but if I would set out a pail of whiskey with a dipper in it on the top of a hemlock stump that grew in front of the tavern it wouldn't be 60 minutes before I could count the whole of them. We both smiled, as it were, at once.

Having asked some other inquires of a mixed nature, I sauntered down to where the race course was. I found the track was about a mile in circumference and of a sandy disposition, fenced in by a cranberry marsh on one side and a brush fence on the other, and in just about a 3-minute condition.

The judge's stand was an ox-cart surrounded on the sides by a hay rigging. The reporters were invited to get into the cart.

One of the horses was a gray mare about the usual stature, not very fat, and laboring under a spring halt which they said she had caught from another horse about 10 days ago. They said she had trotted to a camp meeting last fall inside of a very short time and that her backbone was all gone.

I asked a young man with long yellow hair and bedtick pants on, who was currying the mare, what her pedigree was. With a wink at another feller, he said, "She was got by the Landlord out of a Methodist Minister," and then they both laughed.

I found out by inquiring that her name was "Frying Pan."

The other horse was a red horse, rather hastily constructed, with a spare tail on him which was said to be caused by his trotting so fast on a windy day. I should think he was about 5 feet and a half in height, and of a kicking nature.

They said he was a stranger in these parts and that his right name was "Jew's Harp."

The horses both come up to the score in the immediate vicinity of each other, and got the word to go the first time. The gray mare was drove by Dave Larkin and the horse handled by Ligh Turner.

They trotted sublimely, as close as the Siamese twins — the mare with her head high up and her nose full of wind; the horse was stretched out tight, like a chalk line; they passed half-mile pole simultaneously.

Now the contest became exciting. Dave hollered and Ligh yelled.

On they come, the mare grew higher and the horse grew longer. . . . They made the last turn once. . . . They look like a double team. . . . The excitement grows more intensely. . . . The crowd sways to and fro. . . . The oxcart trembles. . . . They come! They come! . . . Such shouting, such yelling, such swearing, such chawing tobacco . . .

was never heard before. . . . The mare is ahead! . . . No, the horse is ahead! . . . 'Tis even. . . . 'Tis a dead heat. . . . They pass the oxcart. . . . The horse wins by 3 quarters of an inch. . . .

The horses are surrounded by a crowd of men, women and children for the second heat. Each party is sanguinary of success. The betting is 2 quarts of whiskey to anything on the red horse.

At this juncture the gentleman reporter for the *Young Man's Christian Guide* proposed to bet 75 cents that the mare would win the next heat. I took the proposition forthwithly, and the stakes, by mutual consent, was placed in my hat and sot under the cart.

The horses both show signs of distress. The gray mare's ears hang down the side of her head, like two wet rags, and the horse rests his tail on the ground. They go slow back to the distance pole and come up again to the score, as though they were yoked together. Away they go, the horse a little ahead. The horse leads to the half-mile pole.

On the back stretch Dave went at the mare with his long persuader. She trots like lightning; she passed the horse. . . . No, she busts, and before Dave could flatten her down to her work, she broke from the track and trotted clean up to her hips in the cranberry marsh.

The horse come in all alone, trotting fast, and so close down that 2 feet of his tail dragged on the ground.

Jew's Harp won by a quarter of a mile. Thus ended the great race at Sulphur Flats.

When I went to get my hat and stakes neither one of

them was there. I immediately started on foot for Jamaica Rum Four Corners, bareheaded, but fully impressed that, though men and even whiskey might deteriorate, the breed of horses *must* begin to improve in that section of the country in a few days.

CHAPTER SIX

How to Write a Comic Column

"I am in favor of short stories when a man ain't got much to say."

It may look like an easy task to those who never tried it to write a half a column material each week, and it is an easy task to those who never tried it. But to those who have tried it, and who have even succeeded but a few inches, it is a good deal like lifting things that are tied down.

In the first place a comic essay must have a short back, be sharp on the withers, not too long-legged, kind in all harness, hard to scare, and able to show its heels to a road wagon.

The power of a comic essay resides in its idea, either original or admirably stolen, not in its words, strung out lazily like a snake sunning himself in the sand.

It is no place for your short essayer to hide among the debris of abstracted thoughts, or skulk behind a flame-colored paragraph, or doze in recital upon an ebb tide, or hammer out an iron proposition into points more or less dull, or quote Latin or bad French, but he must be as short as a newsboy's prayer, as sudden as the end of a rope, as quick as a sneeze, and as brilliant in his busts as a skyrocket.

All real strength is short; things are broke or histed with a jerk; comic essayers must ram pages into paragraphs; wit or humor is something like ginger pop — there is about as much in the pop that is interesting as there is in the ginger.

These short essays are like buckwheat slapjacks: everybody seems to like them hot, and to get them hot is just where the little joker comes in.

A lukewarm comic essay has no more fun in it than a Dutch conundrum to a man who don't understand the language.

I often get letters from some of our best philanthropists who love me, they say, and who wonder why I don't write some longer things. All I can say to them is that a short-built writer is dull enough, and a long-built one necessarily so. A streak of lazy lightning, a mile long, that anybody can dodge, soon loses all its novelty.

There is a great power in words if you don't hitch too many of them together, but their only power is the interpretation of ideas. The more ginger you can get into the pop the better the dose.

Some men are never so brilliant as when they don't make any remarks, and no man needn't get mad at himself because he has said a good thing without wasting a word.

A comic essayer has got to have a sprinkling of the monkey in him; he must act sensible things strangely. It is not an easy task to be a good monkey, nor will it exactly answer to be an artificial monkey — the deviltry in a monkey is natural and if it wasn't, it wouldn't be funny but ridiculous.

If any of the first-class philanthropists have got any spare capital lying idle that they would like to insert into the comic essay business, I am ready to sell out my small stock, good will and fixtures, and I will quietly go into the frog's hind leg trade. If at the end of 90 days they don't find the silver-plated nonsense business harder to steer than they think it is, I will give them credit for having a good stock of brains or impudence, I don't know which.

A man who is on a journey is expected to go slow and get dull, but if he is on an errand he is expected to be lively. It is justly thus with your long and your close-built writers.

I hope those who take the pains to read this squiblet will give me credit for writing what I think, if it ain't so searching and brilliant, and I would thank those who semi-oftenly advise me to pump more power and doxology into what I write, to purchase me out and set up the hot paragraph trade themselves — and give us wit on the half shell, nitroglycerine humor, fun soaked in camphene, jests crazy to go off at half cock, and raw sense that will make a sawhorse laugh.

I am mad that I ever set sail in the comic essay schooner, to be so often caught on the flats, and if I could get out of it now and have any character at all left, I would grab at the offer.

It is a darn sight easier to write too much than it is too little, and all comic attempts must be quick to win, for folks won't bear but little fooling at once on any subject — and I say bully for you, folks.

When I get hold of an idea I have to let it go out into the world like a bird off from my hand, bareheaded and barefooted, a sort of vagrant.

If I should undertake to dress it up in fine clothes, some folks would say I stole the idea and other folks would say I tried to steal the clothes to dress it in and got cotched at it.

I make no pretentions to literature; I pay no homage to elegant sentences; I had rather be the father of one genuine, original truth, I don't care if it is as humpbacked as a dromedary, than to be the author of a whole volume of glittering cadences, gotten up for wintergreen-eating schoolgirls to nibble on.

Argument ain't my fighting weight. I get along the best by asserting things as they strike me, and I say upwards of four thousand things every year that I can't prove any more than I can prove what melody is.

What little I know about things has been whispered to me by the spirits, or some other romping critters, and is as distinct and beautiful, sometimes to me, as a dream on an empty stomach. It may be all wrong but it is never vicious and thus I conclude it is education.

Now I don't advise anybody else to depend for their learning upon such precarious schoolmasters. The best way is to follow the ruts — they will take you to town just as they did your daddy.

The route that I travel is circuitous and blind sometimes. It has now and then a vista or a landscape in it that is worth to me more than a farm of tillable land, but you can't raise good white beans on a landscape.

Whenever I drop my subject and begin to strut in the suburbs of sentimentality and proverbial pomposity, I always think of a gobble turkey in a barnyard on dress parade, then I try to dismount from the turkey and try to get aboard whatever it was I was talking about.

I am called a "broad" humorist and I am glad of it. There is plenty of narrow humorists in the country without me. There is no greater fun for me than to prick a bladder — windy folks will please make a note of this.

I believe that wisdom can be smuggled into a man's soul by a good-natured proverb better and deeper than it can be mortised in with a wormwood mallet and chisel. And the great desire of my life is to amuse somebody. I had rather be able to set the multiplication table to some lively tune than to have been the author of it.

There is not in this wide world a human, or inhuman, being that I would not rather help than hurt. I find this sentiment in my conscience, or I wouldn't dare claim it, and I know my own conscience better than anybody else does.

So adding it all up, manufacturing fun for other folks's amusement is like hatching out eggs — a sober and steady business. I can steal a good philosophical essay out of some library, but these cussed humorous columns have so much original in them (or ought to) that you can't calculate on them for certain — they are like twins; they can't be had nor can't be stopped.

A cold-blooded philosophic essay is just as easy as turning a grindstone — the reader is obliged to hold their hatchets on, and they are sure to get ground out after a while.

But you can't tell a man when to laugh. He knows what pleases him, just as well as he knows what eats good. You can't play a burnt slapjack, or one that ain't well done onto him.

Price 25 Cents.

JOSH BILLINGS'
Farmer's Allminax

FOR THE YEAR

1870

Being tew years since leap year, and ninety-four years since the Amerikan people left Grate Brittain tew take care ov herself, and started a snug little bizziness ov their own, which I am instrukted tew state, iz payin well.

CONTAINING
all that iz necessary for an Allminax, and a good deal besides.

NEW YORK:
PUBLISHED BY one G. W. CARLETON,
[Fifth Avenue, Broadway, and Madison Square.]
MDCCCLXX.

CHAPTER SEVEN

Uncle Josh Does an Allminax

"In Adam's sin we all jined in."

Josh's Allminax *still make good reading. In them he did his best writing. Here (see opposite page) is the title page of his first one — that of 1870:*

The calendar pages are topped with comic illustrations and running rhymes like these:

He who by farming would get rich,
Must plow, and sow, and dig, and sich
Work hard all day, sleep hard all night
Save every cent, and not get tight.

Bring out your brand new cutter,
And get your gal's consent,
Then hitch up Dobbin, or some other kritter,
And let the animal went.

Now gather round the kitchen fire,
And pile the chunks on higher and higher,
Get out the old fiddle and partners choose,
And shake her down in your cowhide shoes.

April fool was born this month,
A simpleton, but clever;
And though 4000 years of age,
He's just as big a fool as ever.

The column of dates, forecasts, and anniversaries is balanced by a series of maxims and aphorisms. The page opposite the calendar has all manner of observations. One year Josh ran a comment on each of the months:

January

This month was named after one Janus, a sharp-sighted old chap, with a face like a pickax, so he could look both ways at once, back into the old year, and forward into the new one. At the latter part of his life he died of a thaw.

Horoscope for January

The young gentleman born this month will remain a bachelor until his 16 year, and will have curly hair. He will finally settle down still, and marry for life. His father will be a great lover of fast horses. He will live to be over 60 years of age, and die worth about 750 dollars.

The young lady born this month will know how to play on the piano and knit worsted. She will be a blonde, and be nearsighted, and fall in love with great difficulty. She will finally get wedded to the man she marries and her whole life will be easy. If she marries the second time her husband will be a dentist or alderman.

February

This month has but 28 days; the extreme cold weather that prevails has puckered up the month. Once in four years there is a big melt and then the month swells, and has 29 days. This month is looked upon as unpleasant, and it is unpleasant for digging out woodchucks, but for setting in front of the fire, and skinning apples, and snapping the seeds at the gals, it can't be beat.

Horoscope for February

The man born this month will be good-looking but too much prone to toe in when he walks. He will have 2 wives, and a small hand, except when he plays whist, then he will have a big one. His first wife will be cross-eyed, but his second one will be cross all over. He will have 4 children who will all pass through the measles with great credit to themselves and no disgrace to the measles.

The young female born during this month will show great judgment in sorting her lovers, and will finally marry a real estate agent. She will have a few failings; but who cares? She wouldn't be interesting if she didn't. At 28 she will be a widow, and at stated intervals will be inclined to gush a little (for the sake of variety we say, let her gush).

March

This month derives her pedigree from the Danish verb "Whizz," which means to blow, to wheeze, to snort, to pitch in endways and crossways, to shake window blinds, to smash barn doors, to scare pigs, to break clotheslines, to make men swear and women balky. March is principally immense for wind, but where it all comes from, and where it all goes to, are prize conundrums which I can't untangle. Dogs created this month invariably have the bark on.

Horoscope for March

The man born this month will be inclined to blow a little. He will be a domestic man, and will know how to rock the cradle and pare potatoes. He will marry the only daughter of a widow, and will be a good judge of mother-in-laws. He will die about the usual time in life, and leave a house and lot, with a small mortgage on it. He never will run for office, and then will get beat.

The woman who appears this month will be an old maid till she is 20 years old, and then will suddenly put a stop to this kind of business by investing in a young man. She will be a good housekeeper, and know how to make a plum pudding with the plums left out. She will hang on to her beauty till she is about 45; after that she will have to take her chances.

April

April, dear April, chuck full of charms,
Come, come, oh come, to my arms . . .

thus warbled the poet, more than twelve thousand years ago, and he knew his biz; he had the right sting in him; he wasn't none of your pedigree poets, nor dyspepsy poets, nor whiskey poets.

Dandelions planted this month are almost sure to head out, so are toadstools, so are headcheese. This month is also healthy for planting onions; onions are a luxury and are good for a bad breath, or are bad for a good breath, I have forgot which, but either way is right.

Horoscope for April

The man born this month will have a liquid temperament, but not necessarily inclined to liquor. His great aim will be to get married; and he will get his bird by marrying a beautiful and also good-looking wife. They will live happy as two lambs, and leave one son, whom they intended should be President of the United States, but who very wisely concluded to be a merchant tailor.

The lady born this month will have blue eyes, and a full set of teeth. Her heart will be as tender as a porterhouse steak. She will keep a lap dog, who will have weak eyes, and whose Christian name will be Fanny. She will die and leave a bed quilt which will go down to posterity with upwards of 7 hundred blocks in it.

May

May is the belle of the year. She has worn the belt for five thousand years. If May hadn't have been a sensible gal, she would have been spoilt long ago with poetry and stanza.

This is an easy month to fall in love. Our natures are now fully thawed out after the late cold snap and like a little melted brook — begin to look around to find another little melted brook to mix with. Oh! how precious and delightsome is the mix. Hive bees during this month, if you have got some; if not, hive somebody else's.

Horoscope for May

The gentleman who invests his life in this month will

be very quick-tempered, especially when a hornet lights on him in anger. His mother will set a good deal by him, especially when he is in the cradle. He will have the mumps very light, and will spend most of his life intending to marry, but will die at last with a half dozen old maids on his hands. The washwomen will remember him as the man who never wore stiff collars.

The lady born this month will be first a bud, and afterwards a blossom. Her heart will be as full of twitter as a canary bird on a perch. She will have twilight hair. She will have many lovers. She will be reasonably fond of silk clothes, but her great joy will be in a bonnet. She will have as little jealousy as is prudent for a woman to have.

June

June is twin sister to May, lacking a month. She is named after Juno, the spouse of Jupiter, and she was a stirring woman. June is the month of roses and milk. June is the stepmother of good grass butter; she is also great-grandmother of bacon and spinach. June is practically a gusher, and I love to stand one side and let her gush — I have made it a rule never to get in the way of a gush of any kind — I say to everything, gush, oh, gush!

Horoscope for June

The male individual born during June will be one of 7 children, but not the only one. He will have 3 brothers, and one sister, who will marry a Hard-shell Baptist preacher. He will study law, and enter the profession with gilt-edge prospects, but his first client being a counterfeiter, whom he succeeds in getting clear, and receiving 50 dollars counterfeit money for his services, disgusts him with the business.

The female who appears on the platform this month will always have cause to wonder why she did it. Her father will be a schoolteacher, and he will bring her up in the district school business. At 29 years and six months she will marry, and will be well educated in the duties of a wife, for she will understand arithmetic, and parsing, just as easy as falling down the cellar stairs. She will have but one son, and he will be educated off from his feet at an early age.

July

July is the seventh month, which accounts for its being near the middle of the year. It derives its name from "Julios" — a hot old fellow, who settled near the equator at an early day and kept everybody in his neighborhood in a profound sweat. July has many features of *interest,* the *principle* one of which is the payment of semiannual *interest,* by most of the banks, on the first day of the month, upon their *principal.* This is a fine old custom, and I hope it will be kept up, for I own a little bank stock, and take some *interest* in the *principle.*

Horoscope for July

The man mortal who comes to the scratch this month will be a great lover of political life, and after many stormy trips will settle in his native village a constable, elected by 19 majority. He will live to be ripe with old age, and his posterity will wonder how he managed to spend a whole life in politics, and keep out of state prison. (His posterity probably ain't aware that a term in state prison is a good hard-to-run-for-office on.)

The girl born this month will flash like a streak of yellow sunshine. She will be sought after like the balm of many flowers. She will have poetry for breakfast, and spend the rest of the day on zephyrs and chocolate caramels. The man who gets her for a wife will change into a butterfly, and the two will be seen, some sweet night this month, flying away to the song of the crickets.

August

This month, for some reason, has got a hot way of doing things. All nature unties her corsets and loafs by the side of brooks, with stockingless feet, to catch the cool words of singing waters, and watch the bubbles of sweat that rise on the nose of the green frogs, as they set down on themselves, on the moss-upholstered stones.

Butter spreads itself freely during this month. Snakes slip easy, and Cupid crawls behind the shadder of a dying rose and shoots his gun on the gals and boys.

Horoscope for August

The gentleman born this month will have one eye to the main chance, and the other eye on the collaterals. He will be sharper than good cider vinegar, and will go at a transaction like a Scotch terrier at a rathole. He will be as honest as a hornet, and make as few blunders. He will live to be old. His wife will die young — tired out trying to keep up with him.

The feminine creations of this month will be great admirers of the sterner sex. They will fall in love easy, but will make as few blunders as any other women. They will be guided by the impulses of their nature, which in most women is a safer card than their judgments. If I hadn't got one of the best wives that the world has yet produced, I should be inclined to ask (humbly) for one of the *August-as.*

SEPTEMBER

September is a lackadaisical month, mellow as the decayed side of a pumpkin, and as sensitive as a boarding-school miss during her first quarter in French. Nature makes her will this month — hogs root violently — birds hold conventions and adjourn down south — tree toads boost each other up trees and warble some anthems — katydids chew music and spit it out freely, and bullfrogs post their books.

HOROSCOPE FOR SEPTEMBER

The man born this month will be what is called a wit. He will be as full of wit as a bottle of ginger pop. He can't hardly wait to have the cork pulled out, and when the cork is pulled out it will take a quart bowl to hold a half pint of the fizz. He will make jokes which will be as natural as blunders, and will keep his whole family (including the hired girl) betwixt a surprise and a guess. He will have a house full of children, who will be the best jokes he perpetrates.

The lady born this month will be mistress of the situation. She will have many admirers, but will lead them a dusty chase. After a while she will marry, and become as serious as white mice in a wire trap. Her husband will be as proud of her as a second lieutenant of his first epaulets. Her children will be brought up to toe the mark, and though different from all the other women in the neighborhood, she will be admired more than reproved.

October

October is one of the fall months. Adam is said to have fell this month. But such assertions are like standing off a half mile in a cloudy day, and guessing at the number of fleas on a dog — more sincere than certain. The strongest attraction for me in this month is her natural cider; the man who don't admire good natural cider must be a natural born fool.

Prepare for a hard winter during this month by repenting of your sins and getting up a good big woodpile.

Horoscope for October

The male man ushered into existence this month will be of an inquiring mind. The first thing he will inquire for will be some good cider. He will study divinity at first, but will quit that and become a conductor on a railroad; this pays better, and has more promises. He will marry the woman of his choice, which is good, provided the choice is all right. His hair will turn gray before he dies, but after he dyes he will have black hair the rest of his life.

The woman born this month will be short of statue, and acquainted with grief. She will want a great many things, in this world, that ain't handy to be got. She will marry just about the right time, and undertake to live with her mother-in-law, which is a difficult contract to fill. The women born this month are like Rhode Island greenings, ripen slow, and are most delightful away long into winter.

November

Everybody wants to be sassy at November — to turn her the cold shoulder — to nurse all their old aches anew — to look as sour as a potbellied pickle — to hunt for a cat's tail to step at — but I ain't! November is when I harvest my happiness, when I gather into my pious corn-crib the moral sowing of the whole year. I am only sorry for one thing during the month of November, and that is that I am such a poor, weak, uncertain, sinnerly cuss, and that my neighbors ain't much better than I am.

Horoscope for November

The gentleman born this month will be a hard worker, but fond of old wine. He will forget to pay some of his debts, but will have a blue eye, and be a good singer. He will marry between 18 and 45, and be an excellent judge of hash on toast. He will live a great length, and reach death by a circuitous route.

She who comes to see us this month will be as welcome

as a dandelion in the bosom of winter. She will be a dutiful daughter, a warmhearted sister, a tender mother, and a handsome wife — (kind Heaven! send us as many of this sort as is convenient).

DECEMBER

This is the last month in the *Josh Billings' Farmer's Allminax.* Other duties, of a masculine nature, have forced us to haul in our gangplank. We would like to have hung on a month or two longer, and made a big thing of it. We must part, and it is like pulling angleworms out of their holes, almost sure to part the angleworms.

I have taken a contract to remove the mosquitoes from the state of New Jersey to west of the Rocky Mountains to their new reservation, and I am anxious to get the bulk of them started before they thaw out. I may lose my life in the undertaking, but I have been told by good judges, that it is sweet to die for one's country. I can't tell whether this is so or not; I never tried it. Good-by, this cussed mosquito contract is wearing me out.

HOROSCOPE FOR DECEMBER

A man born this month will have a sanguine temperament. He thinks he is in love with every woman he meets, and won't get married till late in life. When he does get wedded, he is a-going to wed a woman who has been playing the same game he has — falling in love with every man she meets. They are both of them going to get cheated the worst way.

The girl born this month, though late in the season, is

a-going to catch up before she gets through. She won't remain single, and is a-going to be a little difficult to manage double. She will see Naples, but is too smart right off on that account. She will admire many men, but will love but one, and that is her husband. If her husband is smart enough to know this, they will travel through life like 2 pigeons.

Also on this page, and scattered through the Allminax, *Josh gave helpful hints and advice of all sorts. Here are some samples:*

How to Cure the Blues

Marry some delicate only daughter of 22 summers (more or less) and take your mother-in-law home with you to board. This will oil the pores of the system and the blues will escape like steam out of the nose of a teakettle.

Or hire out to keep district school for 9 dollars a month and hash around the neighborhood.

Or take a 3-year-old kicking heifer to break to milk. This will open your swearing valves and so hurry the blood that the blues will leave you in disgust and fasten their fangs onto some other fellow. Againly, go down into some marsh in the Kingdom of New Jersey fishing for frogs in the month of August and fish with one hand and slap mosquitoes with the other. The blues will take the hint and vacate your nature like a shooting star.

Domestic Receipts

To find the square root of a hog's nose, turn him into a garden patch.

To enjoy a good reputation, give publicly, and steal privately.

To remove grease from a man's character, let him strike some sudden oil.

To get wrong things out of your child's head — comb it often.

Useful Hints to Boarding House Keepers

Be careful how you soak your mackerel — too much soaking takes the wear out of them.

In selecting a young goose for your table, don't forget to remember that the longer a goose has lived in this world, the more experience he will have when he comes to be chawed.

Keep a cow, and then the milk won't have to be watered but once.

Q: Will you please define suicide?

A: Suicide is cheating the doctors out of a job.

Valuable Advice to Young Sportsmen

The best bait for bed bugs is to sleep three in a bed.

The best kind of a spear for bullfrogging is a four-tined dung fork. When you get the tines all full, shoulder the fork and put for home.

Some Signs of Infallible Weather

When roosters are observed before daylight in the

morning, soaring among the clouds, and uttering lamentations, then look out for some sudden weather, and a severe pucker in the money market.

When you see 13 geese, walking Injun file, and toeing in, you can deliberately bet your last surviving dollar on a hard winter, and a great fluctuation during the next season in the price of cowhide boots.

When spiders are seen climbing up the wall backwards, and frogs cough as though they had the hiccoughs, look out for rain. This is also a sure sign that children will have the measles light.

When hens lay 2 eggs a day, and men cease to brag, and women cease to cackle, then Injun summer draws nigh, and the millennium ain't far off.

If bees hang around their hives and mules are seen in a brown study, a storm of some kind is cooking, and you will notice the market for herring is very cadaverous, and shifty.

Melkisidek Brewster's Lightning Rod

For drawing lightning, these rods have great strength and endurance.

They will draw lightning from the uttermost parts of the earth, or pull it in two.

You may bury one of these rods 10 feet under ground, and lightning will hunt till it finds it.

You might as well undertake to escape natural death, or a constable's warrant, as to escape lightning with one of these rods on your house.

Bury one of Melkisidek's rods, and if you ain't got any house to put it on, you can set it up at the forks of the road, and steal all the lightning in the neighborhood.

Q: Why don't women like an echo?
A: Because it has the last word.

Q: How long can a goose stand on one leg?
A: Try it — that's the way the goose found out.

Q: What is the easiest vittles to digest?
A: A good joke.

WORDS TO HOUSEWIVES

To skin an eel, turn him inside out, and remove the meat with a jack plane.

To make a hoecake, take a hoe and boil it to a thin jell, and then — let her cake.

THINGS WORTH KNOWING

To break a mule — commence with his head.

To get at the solid contents of your wife's tongue, be very sweet with the new schoolmarm in your district.

MORE HINTS TO BOARDING HOUSE KEEPERS

Buckwheat cakes made out of wheat bran cost less and soak up molasses more cheerfully.

Be kind to cockroaches, for they often make a plate of butter last a whole week, and when you pray, always pray for light eaters.

Patents Issued

To Ambrose Griddle, Esq., a patent for a hen's egg, which beats the natural egg for all purposes, except cooking, hatching and eating.

To Ezra Push, Jun., a patent for a one-wheeled velocipede. This wise instrumentality has two handles to it, and is persuaded by taking hold of the handles, and walking between them with a shove motion. If it wasn't a velocipede, it would be an old-fashioned wheelbarrow.

Rathbun's "Old Oaken Bucket Washing Machine"

For washing, bleaching, boiling, wringing, starching, blueing, hanging out, drying, ironing, marking, fluting, and folding clothes, this lovely machine has no competition in the male or female world. This is the only machine in the Western hemisphere that takes the inside cloth off from a man's back on the keen jump, and puts it back again, in 15 minutes, washed, dried, ironed, starched, the buttons sewed on, and the collar turned down. Ask for Rathbun's Old Oaken Bucket Washing Machine, and keep asking till you get it, and when you have got it, hug it to your bosom.

Job Sargent's Cleansing Soap

Job Sargent, being of sound mind, and expressly afraid of the devil, don't hesitate to say that his cleansing soap will take the spots off from everything.

1st, It will remove the spots from a coach dog in 3 days.

2nd, It will take the spots off from a ten of diamonds in 15 minutes.

3rd, Can the leopard change his spots? — I answer it can by using Job Sargent's only cleansing soap.

4th, Persons of spotless reputation, and anxious to keep so, will never be without this soap.

5th, Job Sargent never told a lie — so did George Washington.

Q: Who got the first caning?

A: Abel.

Some Weather: Synopsis of Prognosticated Events

The barometer will rise very sudden this morning at Pordunk, 3 foot, and fall the like amount at Sacramento City. The difficulty in the weather for the last 2 days, which has predominated at Boston and around New Orleans, was owing to the barometer at Pordunk being took down and sent to the blacksmith's shop for repairs.

Clear weather has existed at Goose Creek, and northwest of Montreal, with a growing tendency to wind gustiness.

Probabilities

Ambrosial weather will permeate all around Pordunk for the next 16 months, with rain and snow; and all sorts of stuff in the balance of the United States of America.

The probabilities is that the above probabilities will assimilate themselves to the principal probabilities in the case. If they don't, due notice will be given. In the meantime be calm, be dignified, and don't be scared.

To Contractors

The widow Betsey Brown will receive proposals sealed at her residence No. 86 Hopvine St. for the next 90 days.

Contractors must state their best offers.

Diagrams of the widow's looks can be had at the above No. The widow reserves the privilege of refusing all offers. The highest bidder gets the worm. Agents needn't applicate.

Q: What is a blunderbuss?

A: Kissing the wrong woman.

I never knew, in all my life,
Any man to go crazy,
Who always took things setting down,
And cultivated his lazy.

Q: What's your favorite piece of sculpture?

A: The milestone nearest home.

Q: What's your favorite painters?

A: Sunrise and sunset.

Advice to Young Clergymen

Don't preach the gospel for less than 850 dollars a year, salary payable quarterly in advance.

A congregation who can't afford to pay 850 dollars a year wants a missionary instead of a clergyman.

Be sure and run the church; don't let the church run you. As I said up at the top, get as much of your salary as possible in advance, for I don't know of any debt so hard to collect as a minister's salary after it once gets cold.

FOUND:

A Maltese soprano cat, about 12 months old, singing "Old Hundred" on a picket fence, late last Thursday night; whichever person owns said cat will find him (or her, according to circumstances) in a vacant lot, just back of our house, still beautiful in death.

FOUND:

An old blue cotton umbrella worth nothing, in place of a new one worth 12 dollars and 50 cents. If the person who lost the blue cotton umbrella by finding the other one hasn't had time enough yet to repent of his blunder, 60 days longer will be granted him to weep over the incident.

EXAMINING A PORDUNK VALLEY RAILROAD CONDUCTOR

Have you a gold watch worth 300 dollars? No.

Do you keep a trotter? Not any.

Have you any diamond rings? Nary.

Do you own a fighting dog? Nothing of the sort.

How much bank stock have you got? Not a red.

We shan't want you — the Pordunk Valley Railroad has got done furnishing conductors these things.

Here are some of the plugs for the Allminax. *You may have one guess at who wrote them:*

"Josh Billings' Farmer's Allminax is as full of gems as a diamond necklace, as full of knowledge as Webster's Spelling Book, and as full of cooking and cures as a parson's wife." London *Athenaeum,* May 13, 1869.

"The virtuous thoughts in Josh's Allminax is gin cocktails for the idle, and brandy straights for the vicious." *Atlantic Semi-Monthly,* May 3, 1869.

"In these days of tawdry novels, imbecile poetry, and florid histories, it is charming to take up such a brilliant thing as Josh Billings' Farmer's Allminax, where philosophy and sentiment frolic together, and where wit sits in state, with one arm around the waist of morality." *Omaha Patriot,* July 4, 1869.

"Give me liberty, or give me death, but if I can't have either give me Josh Billings' Allminax for 1870."

"It cured my wife of wanting to die."

"It is like pepper sauce on a hot day."

"My wife brings up her offsprings, and does all her plain sewing by your allminaxes."

"How cool and perforating it is."

"This allminax is as full of sharp things as a hedgehog's back."

"It is a lofty production, full of immense wisdom, graphic delineation, and coruscating generalities."

"Josh Billings' Farmer's Allminax for the year of 1875, is just hatched out; it is like a Thanksgiving pudding, full of rich things; buy it and set down in a corner, and read, and be happy once, if you never are again."

"Saw my right leg off, lift my scalp up, inoculate me

with the contents of a six-shooter, if Josh Billings' Farmer's Allminax for 1875 ain't the bullyest brick the civilized world has ever laid eyes on." *Texas Daily Bandit.*

"Josh Billings' Farmer's Allminax is once more in our midst; like an oyster on the half shell, it can be took standing, sitting down or on the run."

"It's a square deal, chunky and smart." *Texas Blade.*

"We have received Mr. Joshua Billings' Farmer's Allminax for 1876, and shall notice its contents at our very earliest convenience." *Edinburgh Review.*

"It is a joy for the fireside; it is a rest for the weary."

"Aroma of loveliness, perfume of joy, essence of titilation, breath of beauty, seance of bliss, Josh Billings' Allminax for 1877." *Lady's Book.*

CHAPTER EIGHT

Uncle Josh's Zoo

"In the whole history of the world there is but one thing that money cannot buy — the wag of a dog's tail."

Next to trout fishing and horse trading, Josh loved the animal world. From his studies of many types of animals he got much of his wisdom, What this American Aesop tells you about animal nature will shed a lot of light on human nature:

ANGLEWORMS

Angleworms are of earth, earthy, and crawl for a living. They live in rich ground and where angleworms rejoice, corn is sure to be bully.

If you want your angleworms of any size, you must manure your soil. There ain't nothing on earth more miserable to ponder over and weep about than a half-starved angleworm.

It is said by the naturalists that angleworm oil, rubbed on the rear of the neck, will cure a man of lying. I don't believe this unless it kills the man. Death is the only reliable heal for lying that has been discovered yet.

Angleworms are used as an article of diet to catch fish

with. Old fishermen always carry their worms in their mouth.

Angleworms live in a round hole which they fit like a gimlet. They always back into their holes.

The Ant

The ant has no holidays, no eight-hour system, nor never strikes for higher wages. They are cheerful little toilers and have no malice nor back door to their hearts. There is no sedentary loafers among them and you never see one out of a job. They get up early, go to bed late, work all the time and eat on the run.

You never see two ants arguing some foolish question that neither of them don't understand; they don't care whether the moon is inhabited or not; nor whether a fish weighing two pounds put into a pail of water already full will make the pail slop over or weigh more. They ain't hunting after the philosopher's stone or getting crazy over the cause of the sudden earthquake. They don't care whether Jupiter is 30 or 31 millions of miles up in the air nor whether the earth bobs around on its axis or not, so long as it don't bob over their corncrib and spill their barley.

They are simple, little, busy ants, full of faith, working hard, living prudently, committing no sin, praising God by minding their own business, and dying when their time comes, to make room for the next crop of ants.

They are a reproach to the lazy, an encouragement to the industrious, a rebuke to the vicious and a study to the Christian.

Ants have by-laws and a constitution and they mean something. Their laws ain't like our laws, made with a hole in them so that a man can steal a horse and ride through them on a walk. They don't have any legislators that you can buy, nor any judges, lying around on the half shell, ready to be swallowed.

I rather like the ants and think now I shall sell out my money and real estate and join them.

The Bat

The bat is a winged mouse. They live very retired during the day, but at night come out for a frolic. They fly very uncertain and act as though they had taken a little too much gin. They look out of their face like a young owl, and will bite like a snapping turtle. They don't seem to be bird, beast, nor insect, but a kind of live hash made out of all three.

Bed Bugs

I never saw anybody yet but what despised bed bugs. They are the meanest of all crawling, creeping, hopping or biting things. They dassent tackle a man by daylight but sneak in, after dark, and chaw him while he is fast asleep.

A mosquito will fight you in broad daylight, at short range, and give you a chance to knock in his sides; the flea is a game bug and will make a dash at you even in Broadway, but the bed bug is a garroter who waits till you strip and then picks out a mellow place to eat you.

Bed bugs are uncommon smart in a *small* way: one pair

of them will stock a hair mattress in 2 weeks with bugs enough to last a small family a whole year.

Bed bugs when they have grown all they intend to are about the size of a bluejay's eye and have a brown complexion. When they start out to garrote they are as thin as a grease spot and when they get through garroting they are swelled up like a blister. It takes them 3 days to get the swelling out of them.

If bed bugs have any destiny to fill it must be their stomachs, but it seems to me that they must have been made by accident, just like slivers, just to stick into somebody. If they was got up for some wise purpose, they must have took the wrong road, for there can't be any wisdom in chawing a man all night long, and raising a family, besides, to follow the same trade. If there is some wisdom in this, I hope the bed bugs will chaw the folks who can see it, and leave me be because I am one of the heretics.

Flies tickle me but don't make me swear. It takes bed bugs at the hollow of night, a mean, loafing bed bug who steals out of a crack in the wall as silently as the sweat on a dog's nose, and then creeps as soft as a shadow on to the tenderest spot and begins to bore for my oil — it takes one of these foul fiends of blood and midnight to make me swear a word of two syllables.

The Bluejay

The bluejay is the dandy among birds, a feathered fop, a jackanapes by nature, and of no use only to steal corn and eat it on a rail.

The bluejay has no song. They can't sing even "From Greenland's Icy Mountains." But I must say that a flock of them flying among the evergreens on a cold winter's morning are high-colored and easy to look at.

THE BOBOLINK

The bobolink is a black bird with white spots on him. They make their appearance in the Northern states about the 10th of June and commence bobolinking at once.

They inhabit the open land and love a meadow that is a little damp. The female bird don't sing, for the male makes noise enough for the whole family. They have but one song, but they understand that perfectly well. When they sing their mouths get as full of music as a man's does of bones who eats fried herring for breakfast.

Bobolinks are kept in cages and three or four of them in one room make just as much noise as an infant class repeating the multiplication table all at once.

THE BULLHEAD

This remarkable beast of prey dwells in mill ponds and mud puddles, close to the ground, and lives upon anything it can get in its mouth. They have two ugly black thorns sticking out of the sides of their head and are as dangerous to handle as a six-bladed knife with the blades all open at once. They will live, after they are dead, as long as striped snakes.

I don't advise any man to fish for bullheads, but if you feel as though you must, this is the only best way to do it.

Take a dark, hot, drizzly night in the month of June;

steal out quietly from home; tell your folks you are going to the neighbor's to borrow a setting of hen's eggs; find a saw log on the banks of a stagnant mill pond, one end of which lays in the water; drive the mud turtles and water snakes off from the log; straddle the log and let your legs hang down in the water up to your garters; bait your hook with a chunk of old indian rubber shoe; as fast as you pull up the bullheads, take them by the back of the neck and stab their horns into the saw log; when you have got the saw log stuck full, shoulder the log and leave for home; get up the next morning, skin the bullheads and split up the saw log into kindling wood; let your wife cook them for breakfast and swear the whole family to keep dark about it.

This is the only respectable way to have anything to do with bullheads.

The Bumble Bee

The bumble bee is one of nature's secrets. They are born about haying time and are different from any bug I know of. They are biggest when they are first born. They resemble some men in this respect.

The bumble bee is more artistic than the mule and as busy as a choir singer. It is a kind of big fly who goes muttering and swearing around the lots during the summer looking after little boys to sting them, and stealing honey out of the dandelions and thistles. Like the mule, he is mad all the time about something, and don't seem to care a cuss what people think of him.

A schoolboy will study harder any time to find a bumble bee's nest than he will to get his lesson in arithmetic, and when he has found it, and got the honey out of it, and got stung badly into the bargain, he finds there ain't much margin in it. Next to poor molasses, bumble bee honey is the poorest kind of sweetmeats in the market. Bumble bees have always been in fashion, and probably always will be, but where the fun or profit lays in them, I never could cipher out. The profit don't seem to be in the honey, nor in the bumble bee neither. They build their nest in the ground, or anywhere else they take a notion to, and ain't afraid to fight a whole district school if they meddle with them.

I don't blame the bumble bee, nor any other fellow, for defending his sugar — it is the first and last law of nature, and I hope the law won't never run out.

There is one thing about a bumble bee that boys always watch dreadful close, and that is their helm.

The Cat

The cat is called a domestic animal — but I never have been able to tell wherefore. You can't trust one any more than you can a case of the gout. There is only one mortal thing that you can trust a cat with, and come out even, and that is a bar of hard soap. They are as meek as Moses, but as full of deviltry as Judas Iscariot.

They will harvest a dozen young chickens for you, and then steal into the sitting room, as softly as an undertaker, and lay themselves down on the rug at your feet full of injured innocence, and chicken, and dream of their childhood days.

All there is sure about a cat that is domestic, that I know of, is that you can't lose one. They are as hard to lose as a bad reputation. You may send one out of the state, done up in a meal bag and marked C.O.D., and the next morning you will find him, or her, in the same old spot alongside the kitchen stove ready to be stepped on.

Cats often make the night atmosphere melodious with their opera music.

Dogs carry their credentials in their faces and can't hide them, but the bulk of the cat's reputation lays buried in their stomach, as unknown to themselves, as to anybody else.

Cats are very plenty in this world just now. I counted 18 from my boarding house window one moonlight night last summer, and it wasn't a first-rate night for cats neither.

A cat is said to have 9 lives, but I believe they don't have but one square death. It is almost impossible to tell when a cat is dead without the aid of a coroner's jury.

I have only one way myself to judge of a dead cat. If a cat is killed in the fall of the year and thrown over under a snow bank and don't thaw out in the spring and keeps quiet during the summer months and ain't missing when winter sets in again, I have always said, "That cat is dead or is playing the thing dreadful fine."

Speaking of cats, my opinion is, and will continue to be, that the old-fashioned calico-colored cats is the best breed for a man of moderate means who ain't got but little money to put into cats.

They propagate the most intensely and lay around the stove more regular than the Maltese or the brindle kind.

The yellow cat is a fair cat, but they ain't reliable; they are apt to stay out late nights and once in a while get on a bad bust.

Black cats have a way of getting on top of the woodhouse when other folks have gone to bed and singing duets till their voices spoil and their tails swell till it seems as though they must split.

The Cockroach

The cockroach is a bug at large. He is one of the luxuries of civilization. There is no mistaking the fact that he is one of a numerous family and that his attachment to the home of his boyhood speaks louder than thunder for his affectionate and unadulterated nature. He don't leave the place he was born at upon the slightest provocation, like the giddy and vagrant flea, until death (or some vile powder) knocks at his front door. He and his brothers and sisters may be seen with the naked eye, ever and anon, calmly climbing the white sugar bowl or running foot races between the butter plates.

The cockroach is born on the first of May and the first of November, and is ready for use in 15 days from date. They are born from an egg, four from each egg, and consequently they are all of them quadruplets. The maternal bug don't set upon the eggs but leaves them lie around loose, like a pint of spilt mustard seed, and don't seem to care a darn whether they get ripe or not. But I never knew a cockroach egg fail to put in an appearance. They are as sure to hatch out and run as Canada thistles or a bad cold.

The cockroach is of two colors, sorrel and black. They are always on the move. Their food seems to consist not so much in what they eat as what they travel and, often finding them dead in my soup at the boarding house, I have come to the conclusion that they can't swim but they can float.

Every man has a right to pick his playmates but as for me I had rather visit knee deep among cockroaches than to hear the dying embers of a single mosquito's son or to know that there was just one bed bug left in the world and was waiting for my candle to go out and for me to pitch into bed.

N.B. To get rid of cockroaches — sell your house and lot, and flee to the mountains.

The Codfish

The codfish is a child of the ocean. This accounts for their being so salt. They are caught with a hook and line, and bite a steel trap, and hang on like a poor relation. They are good eating for a wet day; they are better than an umbrella to keep a man dry.

Dried codfish is one of the luxuries of life, but codfish three times a day would weaken my confidence in them.

Codfish never venture in fresh water; they would soon spoil if they did.

The codfish is said to be an aristocrat, and to keep aloof from the other fish of his size in the sea, and claims to be a relation of the whales — but this looks rather fishy to me. I have noticed that the codfish always has a stiff upper lip, but I think this is more owing to the bone that is in him than it is to his blood.

The Crow

Next to the monkey, the crow has the most deviltry to spare. They are born very wild, but can be tamed as easy as the goat can, but a tame crow is worse than a sore thumb.

If there is anything about the house that they can't get into it is because the thing ain't big enough. Crows live on what they can steal, and they will steal anything that ain't tied down.

They are fond of meat vittles and are the first to hold an inquest over a departed horse or a still sheep. They are a fine bird to hunt but a hard one to kill. They can see you 2 miles first and will smell a gun right through a mountain.

They are not songsters but what they do sing, they seem to understand thoroughly. Long practice has made them perfect.

I never knew a crow to die a natural death and don't believe they know how.

They are always thin in flesh and are thin inside and out. They are not considered fine eating, although I have read somewhere of boiled crow. But still I never heard of the same man hankering for some boiled crow 2 times.

If I had made the crow I would have made him more honest and not quite so tough.

Devil's Darning Needle

This floating animal is a fly about twenty times as big as a hornet, with a pair of wings on him as much out of proportion to his body as a pair of oars to a shell boat.

They hang around mill ponds in hot weather and when I was a boy if one of them come and sot on the further end of the log where I was a-setting, I always arose and gave him the whole of the log.

They have a body like a piece of wire, sharp at the end, and look as though they might sting a fellow cheerfully, but I believe there is no more sting in them than there is in cold water.

All children are afraid of them and I know of one man now who had rather encounter a wildcat (provided the cat was in the top of a tree and likely to stay there) than to intersect a devil's darning needle.

They derive their name from the shape of their bodies and their general devilish appearance generally.

Dogs

Dogs are not vagabonds by choice and love to belong to somebody. This fact endears them to us and I always rated the dog as about the seventh cousin to the human species. They can't talk but they can lick your hand. This shows that their hearts is in the place where other folks' tongues is.

We have no reliable account of the first dog, and probably shan't of the final one. If Adam kept a terrier, or Eve a poodle, the lapse of ages have washed away the fact. If Noah had a pair of each breed of dogs on board his vessel, and only one pair of fleas, he was well out for dogs and poor out for fleas.

THE YELLOW DOG

The yellow dog has no pedigree; the blood in his veins is as crude as petroleum when it first comes pumping out of the earth, bitter, thick and fiery. He is long and lazily put together, his ears flop when he shacks along the dusty thoroughfare, and his tail is a burden. There is no animation in it. It is worse than a 10 per cent mortage to the rest of his body. Why the yellow dog ain't born discounted is a mystery to me until I ask myself, "Where would you hitch the tin pan to?"—then the folly of a bobtailed yellow dog flashes on my mind.

Ever since this continent was found by Columbus in 1492, and for what I know much time previous to that, the yellow dog has been a vagrant, traveling by moonlight and hungry by nature.

If you speak a kind word to him he thinks it is a hawk in disguise and straddling his tail with both hind legs, he goes suspicious and sideways on his lonesome journey. Mankind has made him a vagabond and life to him is made up of starvation and brickbats.

The yellow dog has but one friend among men and that is the Negro. A common misfortune links them together.

Man's inhumanity is worse than the malice of wild

beasts. A day of reckoning will come, a day of judgment, and I can't tell but what the yellow dog will be there, a mute witness, and then and there will a great problem be solved.

This world is full of great wrongs and the next one will as certainly be as full of great retributions.

I can't endure the sight of oppression; it disgraces my manhood. If I had money enough I would like to buy even all the yellow dogs there is on the bosom of the earth and make them respected and happy.

But I ain't got the money, nor never shall have, but as long as I have strength to steer a goose quill, and blood enough in my heart for ink, I will bid mankind beware of oppression, I don't care whether it is in high places or low, the oppression of caste, the oppression of wealth, or even the low and degrading oppression of a tin pail in hot pursuit of the friendless, yelping yellow dog.

Yellow dogs will sometimes and somewhere have their day, and when the huge piles of brickbats and mountains of old tinware comes into court I want to be there, for I am anxious to know what the line of defense will be.

The Donkey

I have watched the donkey with a great deal of patient anxiety. They are about 3 foot high, and something like 3 foot 6 inches lengthwise. They have a normal appetite, and will eat all the time, and more too. They ain't particular about their vittles, and will try hard to swallow a horseshoe, but they can't do it.

They are set in their ways as a gatepost and are the only live thing that are too much for a club. They will stand more pounding than a sheaf of wet oats without shelling out.

The donkey has 2 ears, and only 1 tail, and the ears are to the rest of their body like two steeples to a church. The donkey is a sober and mysterious cuss.

As a close study, the donkey is as full of interests as a milestone with the letterings all worn off. Donkeys will live forever, or thereabouts, and retain their beauty and intelligence to the last.

The Dove

The dove eats oats and bill and coo. They love each other like a new married couple.

The dove was one of Noah's pets when he sailed. The first dove he sent out of the ark brought back an olive branch and the next time he sent her out she didn't bring back anything. She even forgot to come back herself.

The dove is more ornamental than useful. They are too innocent to be useful. Sometimes too much innocence interferes with business.

I have known half a dozen doves to get into a pie together, and make themselves useful for a few minutes. I don't hate dove pie.

The Bible tells us "to be as wise as a serpent but *harmless* as a dove." This is first-rate advice, but it means live business. Anybody who is as wise as a serpent can afford to be as harmless as a dove. The right mixture of dove and serpent in man's nature is a good dose. If a man has got too much snake in him, he is liable to overdo things, and if he has too much dove in him, he ain't apt to cook things enough.

I wouldn't like any better fun than to live where there wasn't anything else but doves and lambs. But this place ain't laid down on any maps in this world.

Hawks and wolves have made the dove and lamb trade dreadful uncertain.

THE DUCK

The duck is built something like a hen and are an up-and-down flat-footed job. They quack like a root doctor and their bill resembles a veterinary surgeon's.

They have a woven foot and can float on the water as natural as a soap bubble.

They are pretty much all feathers and when the feathers are all removed and their innards out, there is just about as much meat on them as there is on a crookneck squash that has gone to seed.

Wild ducks are very good shooting, and are very good to miss also, unless you understand the business. You should aim about three foot ahead of them and let them fly up to the shot. I have shot at them all day and got nothing but a tail feather now and then. But this satisfies me for I am crazy for all kinds of sport, you know.

When cooked, it will do to call roast duck and apple-sauce easy to contend with. A duck's feather bed is a good place to raise nightmares on.

Ducks are addicted to a wild state of nature, but civilization has did something handsome for them and made them the companions of man and old women.

Sometimes a duck gets lame, and when they do, they lay right down and give it up. There ain't no 2-legged thing on the face of this earth can outlimp a lame duck. You often hear the term "lame duck" applied to some men, and perhaps never knew what it meant. Study nature, and you will find out where the truth comes from.

The Eagle

There is a great deal of poetry in eagles. They can look at the sun without winking; they can split the clouds with their flashing speed; they can pierce the blue ethereal away up ever so far; they can plunge into midnight's black space like a falling star; they can set on a giddy crag four thousand miles high and, looking down onto a green pasture, can tell whether a lamb is fat enough to steal or not.

Jupiter, god of the ancients, had a great taste for eagles, if we can believe what the poets sing. As for me, I have seen the bald-headed eagle and shot them in all their native majesty, and look upon them with the same kind of veneration that I do upon all sheep stealers.

The Eel

The eel will bite a hook as cheerfully as a snapping turtle and hang on like a puppy to an old cowhide boot. They are much easier to get onto a hook than to get off, for when you draw them out of the water they will tie themselves and the fish line into more than 7 hundred dilemmas.

I had just as leaf take a bumble bee off a dandelion as an eel off from a hook.

Fried eels are said to be good, but I always have to shut at least one eye to eat them. I don't know whether an eel is the same as a snake, exactly, but they are near enough to suit me.

Fish and Snakes

Fish and snakes are two things that authors are apt to consider the facts of when they write about them.

I never knew a man yet, not even of first-rate judgment, if he should catch a fish that weighed 4 pounds but would guess he weighed 6, and if he should kill a snake that was 5 feet and 3 inches long would want to swear he was 14 feet long without taking the crooks out of him. This is human nature.

I look upon all things in the Bible with the utmost veneration. I have wondered if Jonah's catching the whale just as he did wasn't some kind of authority for the fish stories of the present days.

If a man in these times should catch a whale as Jonah did he would write an account of it and travel around the country and lecture on it, and when he described the size of that whale, if a man wasn't smart in figgers, he would get a poor idea of the animal's dimensions.

The Flea

The smallest animal of the brute creation and the most

pesky is the flea. They are about the bigness of an onion seed and shine like a brand-new shot. They spring from low places and can spring further and faster than any of the bug-brutes. They bite worse than the mosquito for they bite on a run. One flea will go all over a man's suburbs in 2 minutes and leave him as freckled as the measles.

It is impossible to do anything well with a flea on you except swear, and fleas ain't afraid of that. The only way is to quit business of all kinds and hunt for the flea, and when you have found him, he ain't there. This is one of the flea mysteries — the faculty they have of being entirely lost just as soon as you have found them.

I don't suppose there is ever killed, on an average during any one year, more than 16 fleas in the whole United States of America, unless there is a casualty of some kind. Once in a while there is a dog gets drowned sudden and then there may be a few fleas lost.

They are about as hard to kill as flaxseed is and if you don't mash them up as fine as ground pepper they will start business again, on a smaller capital, just as pestiferous as ever.

The Fly

The fly is a domestic but friendly insect, without brains and without guile, that make their appearance among mankind a good deal as the wind does, "where it listeth."

They are so universal at times that I have thought they didn't wait to be born, but took the first good chance that was offered and come just as they are.

They are said to be male and female, but I don't think they consider the marriage tie binding, for they look so much alike that it would be a great waste of time finding out which was who, and this would lead to never-ending fights — which is the rhubarb of domestic life.

They make their annual visit about the first of May (more or less depending on where you live) but don't get to buzzing good till the center of August. They stay with us until cold weather puts in and leave pretty much as they come.

Many of them are cut off in the flower of their youth, and usefulness, but this don't interfere with their census, for there is another steps right into their place and heirs their property.

Some lose their lives by lighting too near the rim of a toad's nose, and fall in, when the toad gapes, and others get badly stuck by fooling with molasses. Some visit the spiders and are induced to stay.

The fly is no respecter of persons. He lights onto the pouting lips of a sleeping loafer just as easy as he does onto the bosom of the queen of beauty, and will buzz an alderman or a hod carrier if they get in his way.

Flies, morally considered, are like a large share of the rest of human folks — they won't settle on a good healthy spot in a man, not if they can find a spot that is a little raw.

Their principal food is anything. They will pitch into a dead snake, or a quarter of beef, with the same anxiety, and will eat from sunrise till seven o'clock in the evening without getting more than half full.

The fly has a remarkable impoverished memory. You may drive him out of your ear and he will land on your forehead; hit him angrily and he will enter your nose; the oftener you get rid of him in one spot, the more he gets onto another; the only way to inculcate your meaning is to smash him up fine.

Although they hang around saloons a good deal, I never saw a fly the worse for liquor, but I have often seen liquor the worse for flies.

Flies see a great deal of society. They are admitted into all circles and if they remember one half that they see and hear, what a world of funny secrets would unfold! But flies are perfectly honorable and never betray a confidence.

What would some lovers give if they could only get a fly to blab—but a fly is a perfect gentleman. He eats off your plate, enjoys your conversation, sees sights and has more fun, and privileges, than a prime minister, or a dressing maid, but when you come to pump him, he is as dry in the mouth as a salt codfish.

There are some things a fly will blow, but they won't blow a secret.

I don't know of a more happy, whole-souled, honest critter, among the bug persuasion, than a handsome, square-built fly, taking a free ride in Central Park, with the Mayor and his wife, or a free lunch at Delmonico's with the minister from England, and then finishing up the business of the day by sleeping upside down on the ceiling of my lady's bedchamber.

I don't love a fly enough to leave my vittles and fall

down flat on my stomach and worship him, but a fly may come and sit on my nose all day and chaw his cud in silence — if he will only sit still.

The Fox

The fox is a fleshy-minded sinner, and his blandness is too much for the quaintness of the goose, the melancholy reserve of the turkey, or the pompous rhetoric of the rooster. They all kneel to the logic of his tongue and find themselves at rest in his stomach.

He loves lambs and green peas — but will discount the peas rather than lose his dinner — and will go a mile and a half out of his way to be polite to a duck or a gosling.

But the most lively trait of the fox is his cunning. He always pettifogs his own case and wins a great deal oftener than he loses. Foxes are not like men, critters of habit. They never do a thing twice with the same figures, and often alter their mind before they do a thing once. This is the effect of too much genius.

There is this difference between genius and common sense in a fox: Common sense is governed by circumstances, but circumstances is governed by genius.

The fox has no moral honesty, but he has got a great supply of political honesty. If another fox in his parish wants a fat goose, he will work hard and get the goose for him, and then clean the meat all off from the outskirts of the goose for pettifogging the case, and give him the bones, and tell his political friend, with a smile in the left corner of his eye, that "everything is lovely and the goose hangs high."

Foxes have learnt this piety from watching the men get geese from each other, and if animals don't want their piety to get sour, they must keep away from the men weekdays. The fox is too much of a politician to invest his religion in any such indigenous trash. He knows that society has claims on him, for some goose, and expects to have for several more.

Foxes come out of the ground through the instrumentality of a hole, but whether the hole begins at the surface and runs into the mountain, or whether it begins in the mountain and runs to the surface don't make a cussed bit of difference.

But philosophers have argued about this hole business for years. Some of them say it runs in and some of them be darned if it does. While they stand fighting at the mouth of the hole, the fox is stealing their ducks and goslings.

Foxes are like cunning men — they have but few brains and but a small place to keep them in, but what few they have got are like angleworms in hot water — full of anxiety and misery.

Cunning is a branding iron — the letters on it are small but always red-hot.

The Frog

I think I could catch frogs well enough, but I should insist upon their taking themselves off from the hook. I had rather take a boss bumble bee in my hand than a live frog — not because I am afraid the frog would bite but I am afraid of their kicking.

Some people ain't afraid to take anything with their hands — not even an eel — but if I should ever get caught by an eel, if I couldn't settle with him right off, by giving him the hook and line, I would throw the pole into the bargain and put for home.

The frog comes from a pollywog. The pollywog is created by the side of the road, out of thick water, and spends his infancy in pollywogging. After he has got through pollywogging, he turns his attention to bigger things by coming to the conclusion that the best thing he can do is to become a frog.

This is the way the frog first come to be made and pollywogs to be lost.

Now the pollywog leaves the water and spends part of his summers upon land. He generally goes on the jump. Being better at diving than at dodging he often runs his head against sticks and stones that boys throw at him, but his two mortal enemies are the Frenchman and the striped snake. The Frenchman is satisfied with his hind legs but the snake swallows him whole.

I have seen some good time made by a frog and a snake — the snake after the frog and the frog after dear life.

I don't know as the pollywog gains anything by swapping himself off for a frog, unless it is experience, but I never have been able to discover much of any happiness in experience.

The Goat

The goat is a coarse woolen animal. They have a split

hoof and a whole tail, a good appetite, and a sanguine digestion. They swallow what they eat and will eat anything they can bite.

The male goat has two horns on the ridge of his head and a mustache on his bottom lip. He is the plug-ugly of the neighborhood, and will fight anything from an elephant down to his shadow on a dead wall. He strikes from his butt end, instead of the shoulder, and is as likely to hit as a hammer is a nail head. He is a highly seasoned animal, as much so as a pound of asafetida.

Goats are good eating when they are young, but leave off as they get stronger. They are always poor in body but fat in the stomach. What they eat seems to all go to appetite. You might as well agree to fat an indian rubber overshoe by filling it with clam shells as to raise any adipose membrane on the outside bust of a goat. A fat goat would be a literary curiosity.

They use the same dialect as the sheep and the young ones speak the language more fluently than the parents do.

The male goat when he is pensive is a venerable and philosophic-looking old cuss, and wouldn't make a bad professor of arithmetic in some of our colleges. They are handy at living a long time, reaching an advanced age without any definite conclusions.

The milk, which is extracted from the female goat, is excellent to finish up young ones on, but is apt to make them bellicose and fightful. It is not uncommon for a baby, while inhaling this pugnacious fluid, to let off his left collection of digits and catch the nurse on the pinnace of the smeller and tap it for claret. This is a common fact among Irish babies and explains the reason why in afterlife they make such brilliant hits.

The Goose

The goose is a grass animal but don't chaw her cud. They are good livers — about one acre to a goose is enough, although there is some folks who think one goose to 175 acres is nearer right.

Geese stay well — some of our best biographers say 70 years is about right — and grow tough to the last.

They lay one egg at once, about the size of a goose egg, in which the gosling lies hid.

The goose is good eating but not good chawing. The reason of this remains a profound secret to this day.

When the female goose is at work hatching she is a hard bird to please. She riles clear up from the bottom in a minute and will fight a yoke of oxen, if they show her the least bit of sass.

The goose is excellent for feathers which she sheds every year by the handful.

The goose can haul one leg up into its body and stand on the other all day and not touch anything. There ain't but darn few men can do this.

The gosling is the old goose's young child. They are yellow all over and as soft as a ball of worsted. Their feet is wove whole, and they can swim as easy as a drop of castor oil on the water.

The gosling waddles when he walks, and paddles when he swims—he never dives, like a duck, out of sight in the water, but only changes ends.

The goose is different in one respect from the human family, who are said to grow weaker as they grow wiser; a gosling always grows tougher and more foolish.

The Grasshopper

The Bible says, "The grasshopper is a burden," and I never knew the Bible to say anything that wasn't so.

When the grasshop begins to live they are very small, but in a little while there gets to be plenty of them. They only live one year at once, and then go back and begin again. Their best gait is a hop, and with the wind on their quarters they can make some good time.

They are a sure crop to raise, but some years they raise more than others. I have seen some fields so full of them that you couldn't stick another grasshopper in unless you sharpened him off to a point. When they get so very plenty, they are very apt to want to start, and then they become a traveling famine, and leave the road they take as barren as the inside of a country church during a weekday.

Grasshoppers don't seem to be actually necessary for our happiness, but they may be. We don't even know what we want most. I don't want grasshops to give entirely out, not if they are a blessing, but I have thought (to myself) if they would let the grass and cornstalks be, and pitch onto the burdocks and Canada thistles, I would bet a few dollars on the thistles just to encourage the fight, and wouldn't care a cuss if they both got finally licked.

But my best judgment would be to bet on the grass-hops.

Grubworm

The grub is all the fashionable colors except checkered. I never saw a checkered grub so far.

The grub (that I am talking about) boards in old rotten logs and decayed stumps and grubs for a living. They are about one inch in size and are built like a screw. They look for all the world like a short strip of fat pork. They enter rotten wood like an inch screw pursued by a screwdriver.

Some folks can't see any money in a grub but I can.

I have chopped them out of an old stump, the further end of April, and then put them onto a hook and crept down behind a bunch of willows in the meadow and dropped them, kind of natural, into the swift water and in less than 40 seconds have jerked out of the silvery flood 12 ounces of trout and, while he turned purple and gold somersets on the grass, I have had my heart swell up in me like a hallelujah.

I had rather catch a trout in this way than to be President of the United States for the same length of time.

There may not be as much ambition in it, but there is a glory in it as crazy and as safe as soda water.

It don't take much to make me happy, but it will take

more money than any man on this footstool has got to buy out the little stock I always keep on hand.

The Guinea Hen

The guinea hen is a speckled critter, smaller than the goose, and bigger than the wild pigeon. They have a keen eye, a red cockade on their heads, and always walk on a run.

They lay eggs in great profusion, but they lay them so much on the sly that they often can't find them themselves.

They are as freckled as a coach dog, and just about as tough to eat as a half-boiled crow.

They have a voice like a piccolo flute, and for racket, two of them can make a saw that is being filed ashamed of itself.

They are a very shy bird, and the nearer you get to them, the further they get off.

They are more ornamental than useful, but are chiefly good to frighten away hawks. They will see a hawk up in the sky 3 miles and a half off and will begin to holler and make a fuss about it.

The Hawk

The hawk is a carnivorous fowl, and a chickenivorous one, too, every chance he can get. I have seen them shut up their wings and drop down out of the sky like a destroying angel and pick up a young gosling in each hand and soar aloft again pretty quick.

They build their nests out of the reach of civilization so

that no missionary can get to them unless he can climb well. Powder and double B shot is the only thing that will civilize a hawk clear through so that he will stay so and it takes a big charge of this too.

Boiled hawk may be good. I never heard anybody say it wasn't, but I don't hope I shall ever be called upon to decide. To save my life I would eat boiled hawk, but if it tastes as I think it does, I wouldn't ask for a second plate of it.

The Hen

A hen is a darn fool; they was born so by nature. I have seen a hen fly out of a good warm shelter, on the 15th of January, when the snow was 3 foot high, and light on the top of a stone wall and coolly set there and freeze to death.

Nobody but a darn fool would do this, unless it was to save a bet. I have seen a human being do similar things, but they did it to win a bet.

The principal business of an able-bodied hen is to lay eggs, and when she has laid 36 of them, then she is ordained to set still on them until they are born. This is the way young hens first see life.

A hen has to spread herself pretty well to cover 36 eggs, but I have seen her do it and hatch out 36 young hens. When she first walks out with them supporting her, the party looks like a swarm of bumble bees.

There ain't nothing foolish in this but you put 36 white stones under this same hen and she will set there till she hatches out the stones. I don't wish to say that I have seen them *hatch out the stones* but I have seen them set on the stones until I left that neighborhood — which was two years ago — and I don't hesitate to say the hen is still at work on the same job.

There is one thing about a hen that looks like wisdom. They don't cackle much until after they have laid their egg.

I have seen a hen set on 36 duck eggs and hatch the whole of them out and then try to learn them to scratch in the garden. But a duck's foot ain't built right for scratching the ground. It is better composed for scratching the water.

One egg per diem is all that a hen ought to lay, especially new beginners.

As an article of diet there is but few things that surpass cooked hen, if eaten in the days of their youth and innocence. But after they get old and cross they contract a habit of eating tough.

There is a great many breeds of hens, just now, but the old-fashioned speckled hen breed is the most flattering. After she has laid an egg, she ain't afraid to say so, and can outcackle all other breeds. When it comes to scratching up a garden, they are worth two of any other kind. I don't know of any sight that pleases me more than to see an old speckled hen come sputtering off from her nest and pitch, feet first, into a new-made garden.

I suppose if I owned the garden this thing might not look so funny to me, but you see I don't own any garden.

I have sometimes wondered if it wasn't just about as profitable for me to enjoy the scratching up of the garden, and let them other folks who own the hens and the garden do their own getting mad and swearing.

The Hog

There is a great deal of internal revenue in a hog; there ain't much more waste in them than there is in an oyster. Even their tails can be worked up into a whistle.

Hogs are good quiet boarders. They always eat what is set before them and don't ask any foolish questions.

They never have any disease but the measles, and they never have that but once. Once seems to satisfy them.

There is a great many breeds amongst them. Some are a close corporation breed, and some are built more apart like a hemlock slab. Some are full in the face, like a town clock, and some are as long and lean as a cow-catcher with a steel-pointed nose on them.

They can all root well — a hog that can't root well has been made in vain.

They are a short-lived animal and generally die as soon as they get fat.

The hog can be learnt a great many cunning things such as histing the front gate off from the hinges, tipping over the swill barrel, and finding a hole in the fence to get into a cornfield. But there ain't any length to their memory. It is awful hard work for them to find the same hole to get back into, or if you want them to get out again.

Hogs are very contrary, and seldom drive well the

same way you are going. They drive the most the other way. This has never been explained but speaks volumes for the hog.

The Hornet

The hornet is an inflammable bugger, sudden in his impressions and hasty in his conclusion, or end. His natural disposition is a warm cross between red pepper in the pod and fusel oil and his moral bias is, "Get out of my way."

They have a long, black body, divided in the middle by a waist spot, but their physical importance lays at the terminus of their suburb in the shape of a javelin. This javelin is always loaded and stands ready to unload at a minute's warning and enters a man as still as thought, as spry as lightning, and as full of melancholy as the toothache.

Hornets never argue a case. They settle all of their differences of opinion by letting their javelin fly and are as certain to hit as a mule is.

This testy critter lives in congregations numbering about one hundred souls but whether they are male and female or conservative or matched in bonds of wedlock or whether they are Mormons, and a good many of them club together and keep one husband to save expenses, I don't know or don't care.

I have never examined their habits much; I never considered it healthy.

Hornets build their nest whenever they take a notion

to and seldom are disturbed—for what would it profit a man to kill 99 hornets and have the one hundredth one hit him with his javelin?

They build their nests of paper without any windows to them or back doors. They have but one place of admission and the nest is the shape of an overgrown pineapple and is cut up into just as many bedrooms as there is hornets.

It is a very simple thing to make a hornet's nest if you can but I will argue any man 300 dollars he can't build one that he can sell to a hornet for half price.

Hornets are as busy as their second cousins, the bee, but what they are about the Lord only knows. They seem to be busy only just for the sake of working all the time. They are always in as much of a hurry as though they was going to a doctor.

There is lots of human men loafing around blacksmith shops and cider mills all over the country that don't seem to be necessary for anything but to beg plug tobacco and swear and steal watermelons. But you just let the cholera break out once and then you will see the wisdom of having just such men laying around loose; they help count.

Next to the cockroach, who stands at the head, the hornet has got the most waste stomach in reference to the rest of his body than any of the insect population. What on earth does a hornet want so much reserve corps for? I have just thought — to carry his javelin in.

The hornet is an unsocial cuss. He is more haughty than he is proud; he is a thoroughbred bug but his breeding and refinement have made him like some other folks

I know of, dissatisfied with himself and everybody else. Too much good breeding acts this way sometimes.

Hornets are long-lived — I can't state just how long their lives are but I know from instinct and observation that any critter, be he bug or devil, who is mad all the time and stings every good chance he can get, generally outlives all his neighbors.

The only way to get at the exact fighting weight of the hornet is to touch him, let him hit you once with his javelin, and you will be willing to testify in court that somebody run a one-tined pitchfork into you. And as for grit, I will state for the information of those who haven't had a chance to lay in their vermin wisdom as freely as I have, that one single hornet, who feels well, will break up a large camp meeting.

What hornets do for amusement is another question I can't answer. Some of the best-read and heaviest thinkers among the naturalists say they have target excursions and heave their javelins at a mark. But I don't imbibe this assertion raw, for I never knew anybody so bitter at heart as the hornets are to waste a blow.

There is one thing that a hornet does that I will give him credit for in my books — he always attends to his own business and won't allow anybody else to attend to it, and what he does is always a good job. You never see them altering anything; if they make any mistakes it is after dark and ain't seen.

If hornets made half as many blunders as men do, even with their javelins, everybody would laugh at them.

Hornets are clear in another way. They have found out

by trying it that all they can get in this world and brag on is their vittles and clothes and you never see one standing at the corner of a street with a 26-inch face on because some bank has run off and took their money with him.

I will come to a stop by concluding that if hornets was a little more pensive and not so darned peremptory with their javelins they might be guilty of less wisdom but more charity.

The Lamb

The lamb is a juvenile sheep. They are born about the first of March and many of them die just as soon as green peas come. Lamb and green peas are good but not good for the lamb.

When a lamb gets through being a lamb, they immediately become a sheep. This takes all of the sentiment out of them. There ain't much poetry in mutton.

I suppose if I could have my way the lamb would stop growing when he got to be about 8 weeks old. But then, come to think of it, this would make mutton awful scarce. It would also make lambs dreadful plenty. It would also increase wolves much for I have always noticed that just in proportion as lambs get numerous wolves get numerous according.

Lambs are of the male and female persuasion. There are none of the animals that I can remember of now that are of the neuter gender except the mule.

The female lamb is the dearest little package of innocence and beauty known to naturalists. A female lamb is my pride and hope. I love the whole entire congregation of them. The male lamb soon gets rough. They have horns which burst out of their heads and when they get advanced in the journey of life these horns are a hard thing to contradict.

Louse

It is not the most delightful task to write the natural history of the louse. There is any quantity of thoroughbred folks who would consider it a contamination, as black as patent leather, to say louse or even think louse, but a louse is a fact, and all facts are never more at home, nor more unwilling to move, than when they get into the head.

The louse is one of the gems of antiquity. They are worn in the hair and are more ornamental than useful.

Not having any encyclopedia from which to sponge my information, and then pass it off for my own creation, I shall be forced, while talking about the louse, "to fight it out on the line" of observation, and when my knowledge, and experience, gives out, I shall tap my imagination of which I have a crude supply.

The louse is a familiar animal, very sedentary in his habits, not apt to get lost. They can be cultivated without the aid of a guidebook, and with half a chance will multiply and thicken as much as pimples on the goose.

The louse are well enough in their place, and for the sake of variety, perhaps a few of them are just as good as more would be.

In many ways the louse was our great stimulator in

school. There is no ground so fruitful for the full development of this little domestic collateral as a district schoolhouse. While the young idea is breaking its shell and playing hide-and-go-seek on the inside of the dear urchin's skull, the louse is playing tag on the outside—and quite often gets on the schoolmarm.

I have always had a high veneration for the louse, not because I consider them as any evidence of genius, or even neatness, but because they remind me of my boyhood innocence, the days back in the alphabet of memory, when I sat on the flat side of a slab bench and spelt out old Webster with one hand, and stirred the top of my head with the other.

When, in the lapse of time, it comes to be revealed to us, that a single louse, chewing away on the summit of Daniel Webster's head, when he was a little schoolboy, was the telegraphic touch to the wire that bust the first idea in his brain, we shall see the wisdom of the louse, and shan't stick up our nose, until we turn a back somerset, at these venerable soldiers in the grand army of progression.

After we have reached years of discretion, and have got our education, and our characters have got done developing, and we begin to hold office, and are elected Justice of the Peace, for instance, and don't seem to need any more louse to stir us up, it is time enough to be sassy to them.

As for me, there is only one piece (thus far) of vital creation, that I actually *hate,* and that is a bed bug. I simply *despise* snakes, *fear* mosquitoes, *avoid* fleas, don't *associate* with the cockroach, *go around* toads, *back out square* for a hornet.

Nevertheless, moreover, to wit, I must say, even at this day of refinement, and belle lettres, I do actually love to stand on tiptoe and see a romping, red-cheeked, blue-eyed boy, chased up stairs and then out in the garden, and finally caught and throwed, and held firmly between his mother's knees, and see an old, warped, fine-toothed horn comb go and come, half buried through a flood of lawless hair, and drag each trip to the light, a fat and lively louse — and, in conclusion, to hear him pop as mother pins him with her thumbnail fast to the center of the comb. This fills me chuck up to the brim with something, I don't know what the feeling is, perhaps somebody out of a job can tell me.

The Mink

The mink is one of your land and water citizens and can dive deeper, do it quicker, and come out dryer than anything I know of.

His fur is one of the luxuries of the present generation and is worth as much according to its size as one-dollar bills are. He has no strong peculiarity of character except his perfume which is about halfway in its smell between the beaver and the muskrat. He is built long and slim like a little girl's stocking.

They are not handy to catch. I have trapped a good deal for mink and have caught them mighty little, for they are almost as hard to catch in a trap and keep there as a ray of light is. When caught they are skinned whole.

There is some people who have et mink and said it was good, but I wouldn't believe such a man under oath. I et a piece of boiled wildcat once, and that has lasted me ever since, but I never was partial to wild meat anyhow.

I lived 25 years of my life where game of all kinds was plenty. We had bear, possum, buffalo and rattlesnake, and then night we had draw poker and high-low-jack just to waste the time a little.

The Monkey

The monkey is a human being, a little undersized, covered with hair, hitched to a tail, and filled with the devil.

Naturalists will tell you that the monkey is not a human being; he is simply a pun on humanity, a kind of malicious joke of Jupiter's, a libel with a long tail to it, a mysterious mixture of ludicrous mischief and stale humor, a kind of connecting gangplank between man in his dignity and the beast in his darkness.

I have a high opinion of the naturalist, and all kinds of the dictionary fraternity, and touch my hat to them when we meet, and I respect them for what they know but don't worship them for what they don't know.

I don't care what they say, I tell you confidentially, my Christian friend, that you and the monkey are relations. The only fence between the animal and brute folks is instinct and reason, and if the naturalists can't prove that the monkey don't show a single glimmering of reason I say they must step off the monkey's tail and let him eat at the first table.

The monkey is imitative to the highest degree, and imitation is a direct transgression of the law of instinct and is fallow ground within the domain of reason. Instinct don't step one single step aside to smell a flower or pull a cat's tail.

Pure deviltry is the monkey's right bower. Put him in a barber shop and he will lather and try to shave himself and color his mustache. His face is a concentrated dewdrop of mischief. He scratches his head as natural as a schoolboy and undoubtedly for the same reasons.

Monkeys never grow any older in expression. A young monkey looks just like his grandpapa, melted up and born again. They will eat everything that a man will except Bologna sausage; here they show more instinct than reason.

They won't work and they won't play unless they can raise some devil. They are too much like a human being in looks and actions to kill off. It is impossible to gaze at one and get mad at him and it is impossible to laugh at their smirking satanity without getting mad at yourself.

If anybody should make me a present of a monkey I don't know whether I should consider it intended as malice or a joke, but I do know I should send him back by the same person that fetched him to the donor marked in loud italics: *C. O. D.*

There is only one thing that I have a great supply of doubt about and that is his moral stamina. While in the garden of Eden, previous to the time Adam fell, was he strictly on the square or was he just as full of the devil as he is now?

The Mosquito

The best mosquitoes now in market are raised near Bergen Point in the dominion of New Jersey. They grow there very spontaneous and the market for them is very unsteady — the great supply injures the demand. Two hundred and fifty to the square inch is considered a paying crop, although they often beat that.

They don't require any nursing and the poorer the land the bigger the yield.

The mosquito is a short-lived bug but don't waste any time. They are always ready for business and can bite 10 minutes after they are born just as fluently as ever.

The mosquito can be born or not and live and die in a lonesome marsh, 1600 miles from the nearest neighbor, without ever tasting blood and be happy all the time. Or he can get into somebody's bedroom through the keyhole and take his rations regular and sing psalms of praise and glorification.

It don't cost a mosquito much for his board in this world. If he can't find anybody to eat he can set on a blade of swamp meadow grass and live himself to death on the damp fog.

He don't waste any time hunting up his customers and always lights onto a baby first if there is one on the premises. In the dark, still night when everything is as noiseless as a pair of empty slippers, to hear one at the further end of the room slowly but surely working his way to you, singing that same hot old sizzing tune of theirs, and harking to feel the exact spot on your face where they intend to locate, is simply premeditated sorrow to me. I had rather look forward to the time when an elephant was going to step onto me.

The mosquito has no friend and but few associates; even a mule despises them.

Of all things on this earth that travel or set still, for deviltry, there ain't any bug, any beast, or any beastess, that I dread more and love less than I do this same little gray wretch called cursed mosquito.

In fishing for mosquitoes, don't wait for them to bite the second time.

The Mouse

Paradise would not have been thoroughly fitted out without a mouse to dart across the bowers like a shadow, and Eve would never have known how to scream pretty without one of these little teachers.

I should be afraid to buy a house that hadn't a mouse-hole in it. I like to see them shoot out of their hole in the corner, like a wad out of a popgun, and stream across the room, and to hear one nibble in the wainscot in the midst of the night takes the death out of silence.

Mice always move into a new house first and are there ready to receive and welcome the rest of the family.

Mice come into the world four at a time and lay in their little cradles of cotton or wool like bits of rare-done meat for a month with not a rag on them. When they dine they do it just as a family of young pigs does: each one at their own particular spot at the table, and it is seldom that you see better-behaved boarders, or them that understand their business more thoroughly.

The mouse can live anywhere to advantage except in a church. They fat very slow in a church. This goes to show that they can't live on religion any more than a minister can.

The Mule

The mule is half horse and half jackass and then comes to a full stop, nature discovering her mistake.

They weigh more according to their heft than any other critter except a crowbar. They can't hear any quicker nor further than the horse, yet their ears are big enough for snowshoes.

You can trust them with anyone whose life ain't worth more than the mule's. The only way to keep them in a pasture is to turn them in to a meadow joining and let them jump out.

Mules are ready for use just as soon as they will do to abuse. They ain't got any friends and will live on huckleberry brush with an occasional chance at Canada thistles. They are a modern invention. They sell for more money than any other domestic animal. You can't tell their age by looking into their mouths any more than you could a cannon. They never have a disease that a good club won't heal.

Mules are like some men, very corrupt at heart. I've

known them to be good mules for 6 months, just to get a good chance to kick somebody. I never owned one, nor never mean to, unless there is a United States law passed requiring it.

I wouldn't say what I am forced to say against the mule if his birth wasn't an outrage and man wasn't to blame for it. Any man who is willing to drive a mule ought to be exempt by law from running for the legislature.

I heard of a mule who fell off from the tow path on the Erie Canal and sunk. As soon as he touched bottom, he kept on towing the boat to the next station, breathing through his ears, which was out of the water about 2 feet 6 inches. I didn't see this did, but Bill Harding told me of it, and I never knew Bill to lie unless he could make something out of it.

THE PARROT

The parrot is a bird of many colors and inclined to talk. They take holt of things with their foot, and hang on like a pair of pinchers. They are the only bird I know of who can converse in the English language, but like many other new beginners, they can learn to swear the easiest. They are kept as pets, and like all pets, are useless.

In a wild state of nature they may be of some use, but they lose about 90 per cent of their value by civilization. When you come to take 90 per cent off from most anything, except the striped snake, it seems to injure the profits.

I owned a parrot once for about a year, and then gave

him away. I haven't seen the man I give him to since, but I presume he looks upon me as a mean cuss.

If I owned all of the parrots there is in the United States, I would banish them immediately to their native land, with the proviso that they stay there.

The Partridge

The partridge is a kind of wild hen and live in the swamps and on the hillsides that are woody.

In the spring of the year they will drum a tune with their wings on some deserted old log and if you draw nigh unto them to observe the music, they will rise up and cut a hole through the air with a hum like a bullet.

There is no bird can beat a partridge on the wing for 100 yards. I am authorized to bet on this. The partridge is a game bird and are shot on the wing, if they are not missed. It is dreadful natural to miss one on the fly. I have hunted a great deal for partridge and lost a great deal of time at it.

When a brood of young partridge first begin to toddle about with the old bird they look like a lot of last year's chestnut burrs on legs.

The partridge, grouse and pheasant are cousins, and either one of them straddle a gridiron natural enough to have been born there.

Broiled partridge is good if you can get one that was born during the present century, but there is a great many partridges around that was with Noah in the ark and they are as tough to get the meat off of as a horseshoe.

But broiled partridge is better than broiled crow and

I had rather have broiled crow than broiled mule—just for a change.

THE POLECAT

My friend, did you ever examine the fragrant polecat closely?

I guess not—they are a critter who won't bear examining with a microscope.

They are beautiful beings but oh! how deceptive. Their habits are phew! but unique. They build their houses out of earth and the houses have but one door to them—and that is a front door. When they enter their houses they don't shut the door after them.

They are called polecats because it is not convenient to kill them with a club but with a pole—and the longer the pole the more convenient.

I would suggest that the pole be about 365 feet in length if the wind is in the right direction.

When a polecat is walloped with a pole the first thing that he, she, or it does is to embalm the air for many miles in diameter with an acrimonious olfactory refreshment which permeates the ethereal fluid with an entirely original smell.

A polecat will remove the fillings from a hen's egg without breaking a hole in the shell bigger than a fat pea. This is called "sucking eggs."

This is an accomplishment known to humans which is said they have learned from polecats.

Polecats also deal in chickens, young turkeys and young goslings. They won't touch an old goose—they are sound on that question. Man is the only fellow who will attempt to bite into an old goose.

A polecat travels under an alias which is called "*skunk.*" I have caught them in traps. They are easier to get in traps than to get out of it. In doing so the more you shake them up, the more ambrosial they become.

One polecat in a township is enough — especially if the wind is in the right direction.

Poodle

A poodle is a woman's pet, and that makes them kind of sacred, for whatever a woman loves she worships.

I have seen poodles that I almost wanted to swap places with, but the owners of them didn't act to me as though they wanted to trade for anything.

The Porcupine

The porcupine is a kind of thorny woodchuck. They are bigger than a rat and smaller than a calf. They live in the ground and are as prickly all over as a chestnut burr or a case of the hives.

It is said that they have the power of throwing their prickers like a javelin, but this is a smart falsehood.

An old dog won't touch a porcupine any quicker than he would a firebrand but young dogs pitch into them like urchins into a sugar hogshead. The consequence of this is they get their mouths filled with prickers which are bearded and can't back out. A porcupine's quill when it enters goes clean through and comes out on the other side of things.

The porcupine is not bad vittles; their meat tastes like pork and beans with the beans left out.

They have a cute way of stealing apples known only to a few. I have seen them run under an apple tree, roll over on the fruit which has fallen from the tree, then carry off on their prickers a dozen of them. I have often told this story to people, but never got any to believe it yet.

Porcupines have got a destiny to fill. It may be only a hole in the ground, but they can fill that as full as it will hold.

The Possum

The possum is a fellow of the Southern and Western states. He owns a sharp nose, a keen eye, a lean head, a fat body, and a poor tail. He enjoys roots, chickens, grass, eggs, green corn and little mice. He eats what he steals and steals what he eats.

His body is covered with a hairy kind of fur of a dirty white complexion; his feet and fingers resemble the raccoon; his ears are a trifle smaller than the mules; and his tail is as round as an eel and as free from capillariness as the snake's stomach.

The possum's tail bothers me. I have looked at it by the hour; I have studied it and tried to parse it; I have figgered on it as close as I would a proposition in Euclid; I have hung over it as fondly as a chemist; I have fretted and wondered; have got mad, wept and swore; and can't tell to this day why a possum should have a hairless caudal.

If some philosophic mind, out of a present job, will explain this tail to me and show me the mercy of it, I will explain to him, free from cost, the pucker of the persimmon or the vital importance there is in being bowlegged, two mysteries which are only known to the Billings family.

The possum is a lonesome and joyless vagabond, living just near enough to the smoke of a chimney to pick up a transient gosling or a ten-dollar bill or anything else that ain't stuck fast. Even in poor condition, he is as full of fat as a tallow candle, but having et possum and boiled owl, I am full of the opinion that between the two my choice would be never again to take either.

The Quail

The quail is a game bird about one size bigger than the robin and so sudden that they hum when they fly.

They have no song but whistle for music. The tune is solitary and sad.

They are shot on the wing and a man may be good in arithmetic, first rate in parsing, and even be able to preach acceptably, but if he ain't studied quail on the wing, he might as well shoot at a streak of lightning in the sky as at a quail on the go.

Broiled quail, properly supported with jellies, toast and a champagne Charlies, is just the most difficult thing, in my humble opinion, to beat in the whole history of vittles and something to drink.

I am no gourmand, for I can eat bread and milk five days out of seven, and smack my lips after I get through, but if I am asked to eat broiled quail by a friend, with judicious accompaniments, I blush at first, then bow my head, and then smile sweet acquiescence — in other words I always quail before such a request.

The Raccoon and the Pettifogger

The racoon is a resident of the United States of America. He emigrated to this country soon after its discovery by Columbus. He resides among the heavy timber and cultivates the cornfields and neighboring garden vegetables for sustenance — and understands his business.

His family consists of a wife and three children who live with him on the inside of a tree. He can always be found at home during the day, ready to receive calls, but his nights are devoted to looking after his own affairs. He dresses in soft fur and his tail, which is round, has rings on it.

During the winter he ties himself up into a hard knot and lays down by his fireside. When spring opens, he opens and goes out to see how the chickens have wintered.

His life is as free from labor as a new penny and if it wasn't for the dogs and the rest of mankind, the raccoon would find what everybody else has lost — a heaven upon earth. But the dogs tree him and the men skin him, and what there is left of him ain't worth a cuss.

He is not a natural vagabond but loves to be civilized and live among folks; but he has one vice that the smartest missionary on earth can't redeem, and that is the art of stealing.

He is second only to the crow in petit larceny and will

steal what he can't eat or even hide. He will tip over a barrel of applesauce just for the fun of mauling the sauce with his feet; he will pull the plug out of the molasses, not because he loves sugar any better than a young duck, but just to see if the molasses has got a good daub to it.

I have studied animal deviltry for 17 years because the more deviltry in an animal the more human he is. I can't find, by searching the passenger list, that Noah had a coon on board, but I am willing to bet 10 pounds of mutton sausage that Mister Coon and his wife were commuted — by stealing a ride.

I never knew a raccoon to want anything long that he could steal quick.

Anybody who has ever looked a coon right square in the face will bet you a dollar that he is a dead beat or under 500-dollar bond not to go into the business for the next 90 days.

I have had tame coons by the dozen. They are as easy to tame as a child, if you take them young enough, but I can't advise anybody to cultivate coons. They want as much looking after as a blind mule on a towpath and there isn't any more profit in them than there is in a stock dividend on the Erie Railroad.

I never was out of a pet animal since I can remember till now, but I have gone out of the trade forever.

Raccoons live to be 65 years old if they miss the society of men and dogs enough, but there ain't but few of them die of old age. The Northwestern Fur Company are the great undertakers of the coon family.

I feel sorry for coons, for with a trifle more brains, they would make respectable pettifoggers before a Justice of the Peace. But even this would not save them from final perdition.

Nature don't make any mistakes. When she wants a raccoon with rings on his tail, she makes him; and when she wants a pettifogger, she knows how to make him without spoiling a good coon.

Pettifoggers, no doubt, have a destiny to fill. They may enable a Justice of the Peace, in a cloudy day, to know a good deal less of the law than he otherwise would. Still, for all this, if I was obliged to pray for one or the other, I think now I should say, "Give us a little more coon, and a good deal less pettifogger."

If the raccoon would only give his whole attention to politics, there ain't but few could beat him. He is at home on the stump, and many of us, *old coons,* can recollect how, in 1840, with nothing but a hard cider diet, he swept the country, from the north to the south pole, like a cargo of Epsom salts.

Rats

Rats originally come from Norway, and I wish they had originally stayed there. They are about as uncalled for as a pain in the small of the back.

They can be domesticated dreadful easy, that is, as far as getting in cupboards, and eating cheese, and gnawing pie is concerned.

The best way to domesticate them that ever I saw is to

surround them gently with a steel trap. You can reason with them then to great advantage. Pizen is also good for rats; it softens their whole moral natures.

Cats hate rats, and rats hate cats, and — who don't!

I suppose there is between 50 and 60 millions of rats in America (I quote now entirely from memory), and I don't suppose there is a single necessary rat in the whole lot. This shows at a glance how many waste rats there is. Rats enhance in numbers faster than shoe pegs do by machinery. One pair of healthy rats is all that any man wants to start the rat business with, and in 90 days, without any outlay, he will begin to have rats — to turn off.

Rats viewed from any platform you can build are unspeakably cussed, and I would be willing to make any man who would destroy all the rats in the United States a valuable keepsake — say for instance either "The Life and Sufferings of Andy Johnson," in one volume calf-bound, or a receipt to cure the blind staggers.

The Robin

The robin has a red breast. They have a plaintive song and sing as though they was sorry for something. They are natives of the Northern States but go South to winter. They get their name from their great ability for robbing a cherry tree. They can also "robin" a currant bush first rate and are smart on a gooseberry. If a robin can't find anything else to eat, they ain't too fastidious to eat a ripe strawberry.

Four young robins in a nest, that are just hatched out

and still on the half shell, are as ready for dinner as a newsboy is. If anybody goes near their nest their mouths all fly open at once so that you can see clear down to their palates.

If it weren't for the birds I suppose we should all be et up by the caterpillars and snakes but I have thought it wouldn't be anything more than common politeness for the robins to let us have, now and then, just one of our own cherries to see how they taste.

ROOSTERS

There is not on the whole horizon or of live nature a more pleasing and strengthening study than the rooster. This remarkable package of feathers has been for ages food for philosophy as well as the simple, curious mind. They belong to the feathered sect denominated poultry and are the husbands of many wives.

Roosters are the pugilists among the domestic birds; they wear the belt and having no shoulder to strike from, they strike from the heel.

According to profane history the first rooster was formerly a man who came suddenly upon one of the heathen gods at a time when he wasn't prepared to see company and was for that offense rebuilt over into a rooster and forever afterward destined to crow as a kind of warning.

This change from a man accounts for their fighting abilities, and for their politeness to the hens. There is nothing in a man that a woman admires more than his readiness and ability to smash another fellow — and it is just so with a hen. When a rooster gets licked, the hens all march off with the other rooster, even if he ain't half so big or handsome.

It's pluck that wins a hen or a woman.

There is a great variety of pedigree among the rooster race but for steady business give me the old-time dominecker rooster, short-legged, and when they walk, they always strut, their bosoms stuck out like an alderman's abdominal cupboard. This breed is hawk-colored and has a crooked tail on them arched like a sickle and as full of feathers as a new duster.

But when you come right down to grit and throw all outside influence overboard, there ain't nothing on earth, nor under it, that can out-style, out-step, out-brag, or out-pluck a regular Bantam rooster.

They don't weigh more than 30 ounces but they make as much fuss as a ton. I have seen them trying to pick a quarrel with a two-horse wagon and don't think they would hesitate to fight a meetinghouse if it was the least bit sassy to them.

It is more than fun to hear one of these little chevaliers crow; it is like a four-year-old baby trying to sing a line out of *The Star-Spangled Banner.*

The hen partner in this concern is the most exquisite little bouquet of neatness and feathers that the eye ever roosted on. They are as prim as a premature young lady. It is a luxury to watch their daintiness, to see them lay each feather with their bills in its place and preside over themselves with as much pride as a belle before her mirror.

But the consummation is to see the wife a mother, leading out six little chicks a-bugging — six little chicks no bigger than bumble bees.

Roosters do but very little household work. They won't lay any eggs, nor try to hatch any, or see to the young ones. This satisfies me that there is some truth in the mythological account of the rooster's first origin.

You can't get a rooster to pay any attention to a young one; they spend their time in crowing, strutting, and occasionally find a worm, which they make a remarkable fuss over, calling their wives from a distance, apparently to treat them, but just as the hens get there, this elegant and elaborate cuss bends over and gobbles up the morsel.

Just like a man for all the world.

The Game Rooster

Lo and behold the game rooster!

He weighs about 3 pounds and a quarter, more or less, and is ready to fight for a kingdom. He stands up on his feet like a piece of gingerroot with each feather fastened in its place.

His eye gleams in its socket like a solitaire on the queen's finger.

His head is like the snake's head and his beak shines like the point of a dagger.

When he steps, he steps like a bunch of catgut, and his crow is like the young Indian's first whoop of the warpath. His plumage gives back the sunshine like the ruby and amethyst and his legs are all golden.

His gaffs are of burnt steel and his tail and wing feathers are clipped for the battle.

Bring on the other rooster!

The Garter Snake

The garter snake derives his name from the habit he has of slipping up a man's (or woman's) leg and tying himself into an artistic bowknot about his stocking.

This is more ornamental than pleasant, and has been known to result in the death of the snake.

I can imagine several things more pleasant than a live snake festooned around one of my legs. But then I am a nervous individual and when anything begins to crawl around on me promiscuous, I am too apt to inquire into it suddenly.

I suppose there is plenty of stoics would love to have a snake do this, and would pat him on the head, and chuck him under the chin, and such like.

I give all snakes fair notice that they can't garter me and if I couldn't get rid of them any other way, I would dissever myself from the leg and stump it the rest of my days.

But the more I reflect upon these things, the more I think the garter snake is a myth — a kind of inexplicable thing, indescribable, full of mystery, and is a mere type or shadow of the old time-honored garter itself.

There is a great deal of dreamlike mist and wonderment in the garter. They live in poetry and song, and are seldom seen.

The Snipe

The snipe is a gray, mysterious bird, who get up out of low, wet places and get back again quick. They are pure game and are shot on the move. They are as tender to broil as a saddle-rock oyster and eat as easy as sweetmeats.

The snipe has a long bill (about the length of the doctor's) and get a living by thrusting it down into the fat earth and then pumping the juices out with their tongue. I have seen snipe so fat that when they was shot 50 feet in the air and fell to the hard ground, they would split open like an egg. This will sound like a lie to a man who never has seen it done, but after he has seen it he will feel different about it.

The Tree Toad

Did you ever see a tree toad, my Christian friends? If you didn't, come with me next July and I will show you one.

Morally considered, they are like any other toad; physically they ain't. They are about the size of an old-fashioned 25-cent piece — a head on one side of them and a tail on the other.

They are the only kind of toads that can climb with any degree of alacrity, and are the only ones that can sing like a teakettle when she is cooking water.

Tree toads, when they are on a tree or on the top rail of a fence, have the faculty of disguising their personal looks and appearing exactly like the spot where they set.

I have often put my hand on them in getting over a fence. They won't bite nor jaw back but they feel as raw and cold as the yolk of an egg.

A tree toad lives upon flies and such like vittles, but if they can't get them, they will live all summer on a south wind, with an occasional drop of dew to wet his song. They can outdiet any bug or jumping thing I know of.

The Turkey

Roast turkey is good, but turkey with cranberry sauce is better.

The turkey is a sedate person and seldom forgets herself by getting onto a frolic. They are of various colors and lay from 12 to 14 eggs — and they generally lay them where nobody is looking for them but themselves.

Turkeys travel about 9 miles a day, during pleasant weather, in search of their daily bread, and are smart on a grasshopper and red-hot on a cricket.

Wet weather is bad on turkeys. A good smart shower will drown a young one and make an old one look and act as though they had just been pulled out of a swill barrel with a pair of tongs.

The masculine turkey — or gobbler — has seasons of strutting which are immense. I have seen them blow themselves up with sentiments of pride or anger and travel around a red-flannel petticoat hung onto a clothes line just as though they was mad at the petticoat for something it had did or said to them.

The hen turkey always has a lonesome look to me as though she had been abused by somebody.

Turkeys can endure as much cold weather as the vane on a church steeple. I have known them to roost all night on the top limb of an oak tree with the thermometer 20 degrees below zero, and in the morning fly down and wade through the snow in a barnyard to cool off.

P.S. If you can't have cranberry with roast turkey, applesauce will do.

TURTLE

Turtles live in a shell which they get very much attached to. They are not fond of company, and seldom receive visitors in their houses.

Their style is half land and half water. They have some eggs which they lay in some warm sand.

They belong to the class known as "close corporations" and are a hard animal to whip because they always fight under cover.

Turtles are very tough of life and will outlive an indian rubber shoe, and don't seem to grow old any faster than a pavingstone does.

I take a deep interest in all animals and particularly in turtles, and I do hope that the legislature in their wisdom won't pass a law "prohibiting any more turtles."

I regret to hear that in some parts of the country people are in the habit of using turtles to pitch quoits with, but I think this wants an affidavit with a revenue stamp onto it.

The Weasel

The weasel has an eye like a hawk and a tooth like a pickerel.

They can see on all three sides of a right-angle triangle board fence at once, and can bite through a side of sole leather. They always sleep with one eye open, and the other on the wink, and are quicker than spirits of turpentine and a lighted match.

It is no disgrace for a streak of lightning to strike at a weasel and miss. If I owned a weasel lightning might strike at him all day for 50 cents a clap.

I have tried to kill them in a stone wall with a rifle, but they would dodge the ball when it got within 6 inches of them, and stick their heads out of another crack 3 feet further off.

You can't coax one into a trap and keep him there any more than you could catch a ray of light with a knothole.

They ain't useful for but one thing and that is to kill chickens. They will kill 14 chickens in one night, take off the blood and leave the corpses behind.

I hunted 3 weeks for a weasel once (it is now 6 years ago) and knew just where he was all the time. I ain't got him yet. I offered 10 dollars reward for him and hold the stakes yet. Every boy in that neighborhood was after that weasel, night and day, and I had to withdraw the reward to keep from breaking up the district school. The schoolmaster threatened to sue me if I didn't, and I did it, for I hate a lawsuit rather worse than I do a weasel.

A weasel's skin wore on the neck is said will cure the

quinsy sore throat. But the fellow who said this had a sure thing. He knew nobody could catch the weasel.

Weasels have got no wisdom, but have got what is sometimes mistaken for it, they have got cunning.

The Woodcock

The woodcock is one of them kind of birds who can get up from the ground with about as much whizz and about as busy as a firecracker, and fly away as crooked as a corkscrew.

They have a long, slender bill, and a rich brown plumage, and when they light on the ground you lose sight of them as quick as you do a drop of water when it falls into a millpond.

The first thing you generally see of a woodcock is a *whizz* and the last thing is a *whrrrrr.*

How so many of them are killed on the wing is a mystery to me, for it is a quicker job than snatching pennies off a red-hot stove.

I have shot at them often but have never heard of my killing one of them yet.

They are one of the game birds, and many good judges think they are the most elegant vittles that wear feathers.

The Wren

The wren is the smallest thing surrounded with feathers except the hummingbird. He is about the size of a horse chestnut. He is of a dark brown color and builds his nest in knotholes out of bits of sticks.

He is as gritty as a mud pie, and will fight a hen turkey.

Wrens are little pirates. I have seen them drive a bluebird out of his house and set up business on his stock in trade. They lay an egg about the size of a marrowfat pea, and hatch out at least a half dozen children at a setting.

A young wren ain't much bigger and looks very much like a small-sized semicolon.

Wrens are not profitable to eat — I would as soon dress a bumble bee, and one wren pie would use up the whole breed.

CHAPTER NINE

Uncle Josh on Practically Everything

"The recipe for making a good proverb is, take one gallon of truth, boil it down to a pint, sweeten with kindness and lay away to cool."

Action

I don't believe in knocking a man down by inches — if you have anything against him let him have it.

Men take more pride in their judgments than in their actions — but the world don't.

Adversity

Adversity has the same effect on a man that severe training has on the pugilist — it reduces him to his fighting weight.

Advice

It don't pay to give advice: if it succeeds those that take it will take credit for it and if it proves untrue you will be cussed for it.

Before you give a man advice find out what kind will suit him best.

Most people when they come to you for advice, come

to you to have their own opinions strengthened, not corrected.

ANTIQUARIAN

An antiquarian is commonly a clever fellow who can see no value in an iron kettle until time has made it worthless by knocking a hole in the bottom of it.

APPETITE

The best bill of fare I know of is a good appetite.

ARGUMENT

When I hear a man red-hot in argument, I oftener hunt for the lie he is trying to bury than the truth he is trying to dig up.

ARISTOCRAT

An aristocrat is a democrat with his pockets full.

ARMISTICE

Giving the enemy two chances to get licked instead of one.

AUTOBIOGRAPHY

Autobiographies are the most difficult things to write correctly, for there is nothing that a man knows less about than himself.

AUTOCRAT

I had rather be a child again than to be autocrat of the world.

Beauty

Beauty is the melody of the features.

Beauty that don't make a woman vain makes her very beautiful.

Beauty alone won't wear well, and there is a great deal of it that won't *wash* at all and keep its color.

When beauty and good sense join each other, you have got a mixture that will stand both wet and dry weather.

Begging

To learn your offspring to steal, make him beg hard for all that you give him.

Belief

I believe all things that I hear but place my faith and my money in but few.

Almost any fool can prove that the Bible ain't so — it takes a wise man to believe it.

Best Effort

The man who plays his cards for all they are worth is the only one who can afford to be beat.

One of the rarest things that a man ever does is to do the best he can.

Betting

I never bet — not so much because I am afraid I will lose but because I am afraid I will win.

Whenever you hear a man who always wants to bet his "bottom dollar," that is the size of his pile.

Bible

If the Bible ain't an inspired book why don't someone improve on it?

Bigot; Bigotry

Wisdom never has made a bigot, but learning has.

It is impossible for a man of large brains to be a bigot — his brains are always getting outside his creed.

A bigot is a kind of human ram with a good deal of wool over his eyes, but with no horns.

Blame

The quickest way to take the starch out of a man who is always blaming himself is to agree with him. This ain't what he's looking for.

Bliss

Bliss is happiness boiling over and running down both sides of the pot.

Blunder

Most men had rather be charged with malice than with making a blunder.

How natural it is for a man when he makes a mistake to correct it by cussing somebody else for it.

When a man sets down a poor umbrella and takes up a good one, he makes a mistake; but when he sets down a good umbrella and takes up a poor one, he makes a blunder.

Boy

I would rather a boy of mine would be half full of deviltry than chuck-full of gravity—but I ain't got a boy, you know.

Braggart

A braggart is one who pulls his own courage by the nose.

The man who is always telling what he would have done if he had been *there*—never gets *there*.

Brains

A man with a few brains is like a dog with one flea—dreadfully uneasy.

Brains, or something else that is good to think with, are excellent to have. But you want to keep your eyes on them and not let them fool away their time nor yours either.

Bravery

If I was called upon to tell who was the bravest man that ever lived, I would say that it was him who never told a lie.

Breeding

Good breeding is the art of making everybody satisfied with themselves and pleased with you.

Brevity

I don't care how much a man talks—if he will only say it in a few words.

Bribe

The man who will take a bribe will take anything else he can lay his hands on — after dark.

Cant

Cant is the believing too much what we say; hypocrisy, believing too little.

Careful

The time to be carefullest is when we have a hand full of trumps.

Caution

Beware of the man with the half-shut eyes — he ain't dreaming.

Chance

It is one thing to *take* chances and quite another to *find* them.

Character

If you want to get a good general idea of a man's character find out from him what his opinion of his neighbor is.

To remove grease from a man's character, let him strike oil.

It will do to endorse some men, but not their paper, while there are others whose paper is safer to endorse than their character.

To find the true character of a man, study his vices more than his virtues.

Charity

The interest on charity is paid here and the principal in Heaven.

Charity comes from the heart and a gift from the pocket.

He that gives nothing away while living, dies a bankrupt, and his estate is generally settled by his heirs, a good deal as the crows settle a dead horse, by pitching into the remains.

Chastity

Chastity is so much an icicle that it ain't quite safe to let the sun shine on it.

Cheat

The easiest man in the world to cheat is the man who is trying to cheat someone else.

A man that ain't never been cheated, don't know so much as he will some day before long, perhaps.

Children

To bring up a child in the way he should go, travel that way yourself once in a while.

Precocious children are like peas in February — either forced or out of their latitude.

Christian

No man can be a good Christian who knows his neighbor better than himself.

Circumstances

Men can't make circumstances but he can take them by the horns instead of the tail.

Civility

I hope I shall never have so much reputation that I shan't feel obliged to be civil.

Civilization

I don't think the world has any civilization to spare, but I think she has more than she can manage well.

Clubs

Clubs are places where most people go to get rid of themselves.

Common People

I have learned more from the common people than I have from the uncommon ones — the common people trust to their instincts, while the uncommon ones are ever trying to prove something they don't understand.

Common Sense

Common sense is the vernacular of truth.

Learning is the art of knowing how to use common sense to advantage.

It requires a great deal of common sense to know when we are played out, and an equal amount of philosophy to admit it.

Common sense can be improved upon by education —

genius can too, some, but not much. Education galls genius like a bad setting harness.

Compliments

Compliments, to be valuable, must be false; truthful ones are of no use to anyone.

Compromise

It is better to give a man two thirds of the road than to quarrel with him, but to give him the whole is as much an insult to him as to yourself.

Conquest

It is a crime to steal a dollar, but to steal a whole country, and its people, is conquest.

Conscience

Conscience is our private secretary.

A man's conscience is the only thing that he can be left alone with with reasonable safety.

Conservatism

Conservatism is a bag with a hole in it; radicalism is a hole with a bag in it.

If a man is right he can't be too radical; if he is wrong, he can't be too conservative.

All conservatives have once been radicals, and generally have more policy than principle.

Consideration

Give everyone you meet the time of day and half the

road, and if that don't make him civil, don't waste any more fragrance on the cuss.

CONTEMPT

Men will forget injuries easier than contempt — they had rather be hated than not noticed.

CONTENTMENT

When a man gets perfectly contented, he and a clam are first cousins. When he doesn't want anything more, he is like a raccoon with his guts full of green corn.

CONTRARINESS

Some folks are so contrary that if they fell in a river, they'd insist on floating upstream.

COURAGE

Courage without discretion is a ram with horns on both ends — he will have more fights on hand than he can well attend to.

COWARDS

Cowards are not so from choice — there are none that regret it more than they do.

CREDIT

Credit — like chastity — can stand temptation better than it can stand suspicion.

CREED

If a man can reach heaven on his creed, the road to the other place might as well be fenced up — it won't be needed.

The best creeds we can have is charity toward the creeds of others.

Critics, Criticism

Most people are more afraid of the criticism of the world than of the judgments of heaven.

When an individual ain't got the ability to criticize judiciously, he damns indiscriminately.

To be a good critic demands more brains and judgment than most men possess.

Crowds

I hate a crowd because crowds are made up of people who ain't of much account only to help make up a crowd.

Cunning

You may be more cunning than most men but you ain't more cunning than all men.

Never teach your child to be cunning for you may be certain you will be one of the very first victims of his shrewdness.

Curiosity

The human mind is full of curiosity but it don't love to be taught.

There is one kind of curiosity that prompts us to stick our noses into things for the purpose of smelling.

Curiosity is the same in all people — the vulgar stare and the refined peek through a crack.

Custom

Custom often outranks law and gospel.

CYNIC

A cynic is like a toothless old bull terrior — always growling but never fighting.

DEBT

Debt is a trap which a man sets and baits himself, then deliberately gets into.

"Time is money" — many people take this saying in its literal sense and undertake to pay their debts with it.

Two kinds of men I don't care to meet when in a hurry: men whom I owe and men who want to owe me.

One of the hardest men in the world to collect a debt off of is one who is willing to pay but never ready.

If I had the privilege of making the Eleventh Commandment it would be this — *owe no man.*

DECEIT

Deceit is a dead wasp with a live tail.

DESPAIR

To never despair may be godlike but it ain't human.

DEVIL

The devil owes most of his success to the fact that he is always on hand.

The devil never keeps his own promises but always makes us keep ours.

The devil holds poor cards but he plays them mighty well.

The devil always keeps the guideboards that lead to his dominion fresh-painted and in good order.

The devil never offers to go into partnership with a busy man.

The devil never wants any better show than "I'll see you later."

Difficulties

In youth we run into difficulties; in old age difficulties run into us.

Digestion

I have finally come to the conclusion that a good reliable set of bowels is worth more to a man than any quantity of wisdom.

Dignity

Dignity is wisdom in tights.

Discipline

Discipline is the spinal column of success.

Dispatch

Dispatch has done all the great things in the world, while hurry has been at work at the small ones, and ain't got through yet.

Doctor

When a doctor looks me square in the face and can't see no money in me, then I am happy.

Dreams

I can trace most of my dreams to late hot terrapin suppers and champagne Charlies.

EDUCATION

Give a smart child a pack of cards and a spelling book, and he will learn to play a good game of high-low-jack before he can spell a word of two syllables.

ENEMIES

To pass through this life lively and safely a man should have at least three enemies to one true friend.

The worst enemy a man has got is himself; the next worst is his brother-in-law.

ENJOYMENT

Put not off till tomorrow what can be enjoyed today.

ENOUGH

Enough is just a little more.

ENTHUSIAST

An enthusiast believes about four times as much as he can prove and can prove about four times as much as anybody else believes.

ENVY

Show me what a man envies the least in others and I will show you what he has got the most of himself.

Envy is not such a bad passion when it prompts us to build our chimneys higher than our neighbors, but when it prompts us to shut off his draft it is an awful mean one.

The best condition in life is not to be so rich as to be envied nor so poor as to be damned.

Eternity

Time is measured, eternity grows no older.

Evolution

I haven't much doubt that man sprang from the monkey, but what bothers me is where the cussed monkey sprang from.

Exaggeration

There are people who exaggerate so much that they can't tell the truth without lying.

Executive Ability

Men of few but active brains have the best executive ability — their brains are like a bullet, go straight for the bull's-eye.

Experience

Experience is a grindstone and it is lucky for us if we can get brightened by it — not ground.

There is nothing so easy to learn as experience and nothing so hard to apply.

I have lived in this world just long enough to look carefully the second time into things that I am the most certain of the first time.

Experience increases our wisdom but don't decrease our follies.

Experience makes more timid men than it does wise ones.

Failure

When a man gets going downhill, it seems that everything was greased for the occasion.

Faith

Faith is the soul riding at anchor.

Faith won't make a man virtuous, but it makes what virtues he has got red-hot. If I couldn't have but one of the moral attributes, I would take faith — *red-hot faith I mean.*

It costs a great deal to know all about things, and then you ain't certain, but faith is cheap, and don't make any blunders.

I haven't much faith in man, not because he can't do well, but because he won't.

Fall of Man

God made man on purpose to fall that he might get up and be somebody on his own hook.

Fame

Fame is climbing a greasy pole for $10 and ruining trousers worth $15.

Fame consists in being praised wrongfully while you live and being damned incorrectly when you are dead.

Familiarity

"Familiarity breeds contempt" — only applies to men, not to hot buckwheat cakes well buttered and maple-sugared.

Fanaticism

Fanaticism is born in the heart but never gets to be fatal until it reaches the head.

A fanatic is a lunatic on a furlough which he is liable to forfeit at any time.

Fancy

Fancy is the flirtation of truth.

Fashion

If it wasn't for fashion a large share of the world wouldn't know what kind of clothes to wear to be comfortable.

Faults

About the last thing a man does to correct his faults is to quit them.

Fear

Fear controls more souls than all the other passions do.

Fib

A fib is a lie painted in water colors.

Fiction

Fiction is a lie with holiday clothes on.

Fiction is a kind of halfway house between the temples of Truth and Falsehood where the good and bad meet to lie a little.

Fights

All fights to produce any moral advantage should end in

victory to one side or the other. You will always see dogs renew a drawn battle every time they meet.

Whenever I see a man anxious to get into a fight that don't belong to him, I am always anxious to have him, for I know he is certain to be the worst whipped man in the party.

I don't believe in fighting — I am solemnly against it. But if a man gets to fighting, I am also solemnly against his getting licked. After the fight is once opened, all the virtue there is in it is to lick the other party.

Fireside

Out in the world men show us two sides of their character — by the fireside only one.

Fishing

It is hard work when we see a man catching fish out of a hole to keep from baiting our hook and throwing in there too.

Flattery

There is no servitude so oppressive as to be obliged to flatter those whom we don't respect enough to praise.

Flattery is like cologne water, to be smelt, not swallowed.

Men had rather be flattered for possessing what they don't have than to be praised for having what they possess.

Custom has made flattery almost necessary, but never can make it respectable.

You can't flatter the wise and it don't pay to flatter fools.

FOLLIES

We never outgrow our follies — we only alter them.

Every man has his follies — and often they are the most interesting things he has got.

FOOLS

Only fools build air castles and attempt to live in them.

A learned fool is one who has read everything and remembered it.

When Nature undertakes to make a fool, she hits the mark the first time.

There are two kinds of fools: those who can't change their opinions and those who won't.

The best way to convince a fool that he is wrong is to let him have his own way.

A fool is not necessarily a man without any sense but one without the right kind of sense.

Take all of the fools and good luck out of the world and it would bother many of us to get a living.

FORTUNE

We all believe that we are the especial favorites of fortune — but fortune don't believe any such thing.

FREE LOVE

Free love is the science of loving somebody else's wife more than you do your own and trying to preserve a good average — it can't be did.

Friends; Friendship

Friendship is like earthenware, once broken it can be mended; love is like a mirror, once broken that ends it.

He who ain't got an enemy on earth can't show a friend that will stick to him through thick and thin.

There is no better evidence of friendship than to speak of a man's vices to his face and of his virtues to his back.

Fun

There ain't much fun in physic but there is a good deal of physic in fun.

Fun is the pepper-and-salt of everyday life, and all the really wise men who have lived have used it freely for seasoning.

Generosity

Generosity is the good a man does without being able to give any reason for it.

Genius

Genius is the faculty of doing a thing that nobody supposed could be done at all.

Genius ain't anything more than elegant common sense.

Talent must have memory; genius don't require it.

Common sense is governed by circumstances, but circumstances are governed by genius.

Genius learns from nature; talent from books.

Men of genius are scarce, but men of genius who use their genius for the benefit of the world are scarcer.

Gifts

Giving presents with the hope of receiving them is like swapping skim milk for milk that has been skimmed.

Glutton

A glutton is a man with a drunken appetite.

Good Nature

Good nature is the daily bread of life.

Great Men

Great men should only allow their most trusty friends to see them in moments of relaxation.

Grip

Let us cultivate our grip and let the grab take care of itself.

Grouches

I have heard people who couldn't say "Good Morning" without biting off both ends of the sentence.

Guessing

In a world where there is at least five false things to one that is true, guessing is poor business.

Handsome

If you are handsome, cultivate your boots; if you are homely, hoe your brain.

Happiness

It don't take much to make me happy, but it will take

more than any man on this footstool has got to buy out the little stock I always keep on hand.

I have found that happiness consists in working busy 12 hours, sleeping 8 hours, and playing checkers 4 hours out of the 24.

The happiest time in any man's life is when he is in red-hot pursuit of a dollar with a reasonable prospect of overtaking it.

Hash

Hash is a boarding house confidence game.

To make boarding house hash, take a little of everything, a good deal of nothing, throw in a chunk of something, jam to a mix, cook over a cold fire, season with hair pins, and serve it on the hump.

Hate

I like a good hater, but I want him to give reasons.

There's no man a-going to reach the highest round in the literary ladder unless he is a good hater — and can give unanswerable reasons for it.

Head

In the desperate struggle of life one head will wear out two hearts.

Health

When a man loses his health, then he first begins to take good care of it.

Heart

I have heard a good deal said about broken hearts and there may be a few of them, but my experience is that next to the gizzard, the heart is the toughest piece of meat in the whole critter.

The heart is wife of the head — and a wife is most persuasive when she wants something.

Heaven

There are people who, if they ever reach heaven, will commence at once looking for their own set.

Help

Men can get along without the help of a man, but man cannot get along without the aid of men.

Henpecked

If a man starts life by being the first lieutenant in his own family, he needn't look for promotion.

Hermits

When a man gets disgusted with the world and decides to withdraw from it, the world very kindly lets him go.

History

The history of a nation is the biography of its people.

Honesty

Honest men are scarce and going to get scarcer.

We are told that "an honest man is the noblest work of God" — a large share of the first edition must still be in the author's hands.

The hardest man in the world to cheat is the man who is honest with himself.

The man who has never been tempted don't know how dishonest he is.

If you can't trust a man for the full amount, let him skip.

The man who is strictly honest and no more has no more to brag about than a pair of scales.

There are more people in the world honest by *policy* than from *principle*.

As good a way as I know to get at any man's honesty is to divide what he claims to have by four, and then guess at what's left.

Honesty is a principle; honor a sentiment.

Honesty has been preached more and practiced less than any other two virtues.

Hope

The man who is hunting for some forlorn hope to fight for generally finds it.

I never knew a man who lived on hope but what spent his old age at somebody else's expense.

In forlorn hope a woman's wit is always worth more than a man's judgment.

Hope is a draft on futurity — sometimes honored but generally extended.

Hope hunts up the customers and Debt skins them.

Hope is a hen that lays more eggs than she can hatch out.

Horse Sense

If we could swap two thirds of the learning off for good horse sense, it would be a clever dicker to make.

Horse Trading

Anybody who can swap horses, or catch fish, and not lie about it, is just about as pious as men ever get to be in this world.

Before you buy a horse look him over close, but don't examine him much afterwards, for fear you may come across something that you are looking for. This is a good rule to follow when you take a wife.

Human Nature

The excellence of human nature consists in lifting the greatest amount of sorrow with the least amount of grin.

Study the heart if you want to learn human nature — there ain't none in the head.

Humbugs

If you want to get the lasting confidence of people, treat them honestly; if you want to get their money, humbug them.

A humbug, like a bladder, is good for nothing till it is blown up, and then ain't good for nothing after it is pricked.

Humor

Humor is the offspring of truth — its only malice is to make ridiculous things more ridiculous.

If you expect to succeed as a humorist, you must make people think first and laugh afterwards, and not laugh first and think afterwards — what a fool they have made of themselves.

Let me make the taffy for a people and I don't care who makes their bread.

Even the truth has a ridiculous side to it, and he who can make us laugh at it is the best philosopher.

HURRY

Hurry has the forelegs of a rabbit and the hind legs of a turtle.

HYPOCRITE

It takes more talent to be a successful hypocrite than it does to be a Christian.

I have seen hypocrisy that was so artful that it was good judgment to be deceived by it.

IDLENESS

The devil enters the idle man's house without knocking.

IGNORANCE

Ignorance is the wet nurse of prejudice.

It ain't so much ignorance that ails mankind as it is knowing so much that ain't so.

IMAGINATION

Imagination without taste is a nightmare of the mind.

Lots of folks mistake their imagination for their memory.

A man without imagination is just right for a hitching post.

IMITATION

All imitations must be far superior to the original to equal it.

IMPORTANCE

There is nothing a man makes as many mistakes about as his own importance and nothing that the world makes so few.

The art of becoming important is not to overrate ourselves but to cause others to do it.

INNOCENT

The truly innocent are those who not only are guiltless themselves but who think others are.

INTELLIGENCE

Intelligence without virtue is a head without a heart.

INVENTION

"Necessity is the mother of invention"—and "Patent Right" is the father.

JEALOUSY

Jealousy is a bitter root that we keep to gnaw on secretly.

JOKE

A good joke is a silver-coated pill that frolics and physics on the run.

A good joke is like a pin, it has got to have a head on it as well as a point.

A bad joke is like a bad egg—all the worse for having been cracked.

A practical joke is like a fall on the ice—there may be fun in it but the one that falls can't see it.

Joy

Joy will make a man change ends quicker than sorrow.

Judgment

It requires more good judgment to know when to talk than what to say.

Justice

Justice is the religion of the head.

Civilization has made justice one of the luxuries for which we have to pay the highest price.

Know Thyself

If I knew myself less I might have more faith in the sincerity of mankind.

It is not only the most difficult thing to know oneself, but the most inconvenient one, too.

Knowledge

It is better to know nothing than to know what ain't so.

It is dreadful easy to mistake what we think for what we know.

Mankind is divided this way: one who knows more than he can tell and nine who can tell more than they know.

Laughter

Laugh every chance you can get but don't laugh unless you feel like it, for there ain't nothing in this world more hearty than a good honest laugh nor nothing more hollow than a heartless one.

I enjoy a good laugh — one that rushes out of a man's soul like the breaking up of a Sunday School.

LAW

Good laws execute themselves; bad laws are their own executioneers.

No horse is safe without tying — and less are men.

Going to law is like skinning a fresh milk cow for the hide and giving the meat to the lawyers.

Take man, from Adam down to April Fool, and I would respectfully ask, Is there a single passion of his nature, up to date, that you can take the halter of law off from and turn it out to grass?

LEARNING

Learning is the tool — wisdom and wit the finisher.

Learning sleeps and snores in libraries, but wisdom is everywhere, wide awake, on tiptoes.

When a man of learning talks he makes us wonder, but a wise man makes us think.

LIBERTY

Like health and money, we only know the real value of liberty when we have lost it.

Liberty is giving up of certain natural rights for the sake of preserving a balance.

There is no liberty without restraint.

True liberty consists in making good laws — and then obeying them!

The chains of slavery are none the less galling for being golden.

Liberty and laws are inseparable.

LIES, LIARS

A lie is quick of tongue and nimble of foot, and gets a long start of the truth, but at the finish truth comes jogging in always the winner of the race.

A lie will die a natural death in half the time it takes to kill it.

A lie once told is comparatively harmless — it is the editions of it that work the mischief.

A lie is the cowardice of truth.

Real good lies are getting scarce.

Lies, like illegitimate children, are liable to call a man "Father" when he least expects it.

White lies are said to be innocent but I am satisfied that any man who will lie for fun, after a while will lie for wages.

I have heard lies so well told that a man would almost be a fool not to believe them.

Lying is like trying to hide in a fog: if you move about you are in danger of bumping your head against the truth, and as soon as the fog blows off you are gone anyhow.

A lie is like a cat, it never comes to you in a straight line.

LIFE

Life consists not in holding good cards but in playing those you do hold well.

LISTENER

A good listener is the hardest man to beat — he sees your cards and conceals his own.

Living

The world owes everyone a living—after they have earned it.

Love

Love makes a fool sober and a wise man frisky.

Love is like the measles—we can't have it bad but once and the later in life we have it the tougher it goes with us.

The best cure for love is to live on it.

One way to define love is that it makes us feel funny and act foolish.

Luck

If we were always in luck, we would soon question our mortality.

As long as we are lucky we attribute it to our smartness—our bad luck we give the gods credit for.

Take all the good luck out of the world and millionaires and heroes would be dreadfully scarce.

Bad luck isn't set for a man like a trap but there are people who if there is any lying around loose will get one foot in it.

Luxury

It is but a step forward from hoecake to plum pudding, but it is a mile and a half, by the nearest road, when we have to go back again.

Man

Man is an animal that can be found most generally at home — when he ain't wanted.

Men live to a ripe old age by keeping green.

Man has lifted himself out of barbarism by the hair of his own head and, in the meantime, has run the whole world so deeply in debt that if it was put up at auction to-morrow, it wouldn't bring more than 17 cents on the dollar.

If a man wants to get at his actual dimensions, let him visit a graveyard.

A man with one idea puts me in mind of an old goose trying to hatch out a paving block.

My opinion of mankind as a brilliant success needs a good deal of nursing.

Men mourn for what they've lost; women for what they haven't got.

Men live sometimes till they are 80 and destroy the time a good deal as follows: the first 30 years they spend throwing stones at a mark; the second 30 they spend in examining the mark to see where the stones hit; and the remainder is divided in cussing the stone-throwing business and nursing the rheumatism.

Man is a 2-legged fellow, fond of the marvelous, sharp at a dicker, vain of his guesses, and weak in the knees.

If mankind could have its own way for three hundred years, there would not be one of them left on the face of the earth, and not much of the earth left neither.

Mankind generally admits that the world revolves on

its axis. The only great mistake is that each one seems to think he is the axis.

MAN ABOUT TOWN

A man about town is one who pays cash for everything except his debts.

MEANNESS

There are two parties to every mean act — the one who commits it and the one who don't condemn it.

METAPHYSICS

Metaphysics is the science of proving what we don't understand.

MIND

The mind is like a piece of land that, to be useful, must be manured with learning, plowed with energy, sown with virtue and harvested with economy.

There are four styles of mind: them who know it *is* so; them who know it *ain't* so; them who split the difference and guess at it; and, them who don't care a damn which way it is.

MISFORTUNE

If we could only bear our misfortunes as resolutely as we can the misfortunes of others, we should be philosophers that it would do to brag on.

MONEY

When I was young I thought all money spent was well invested, but as I get older I cipher different.

Money never made a man disgraceful but men have often made money disgraceful.

In money interest follows the principal; in morals principle often follows the interest.

A pocketbook with nothing in it is emptier than a knot-hole.

Money ain't accumulated so much to satisfy wants as to create them.

Money will buy a pretty good dog but it won't buy the wag of his tail.

Mother-in-law

There is one advantage in having a mother-in-law in the family . . . I forgot what the advantage is.

Mystery

Mankind had rather suspect something than to know it.

Nationality

Put an Englishman into the Garden of Eden and he would find fault with the whole concern; put a Yankee in it and he would see where he could alter it to advantage; put an Irishman in and he would want to boss it; put a Dutchman in and he would proceed to plant it.

Necessary Man

Just as soon as people become necessary, they become tyrants.

Mankind would be a happy and well-governed people if they would only let their necessities make laws for their wants.

Nincompoop

A nincompoop is a cross between a little fool and a less one — with the less predominating.

Nonsense

Good nonsense is good sense in disguise.

Notoriety

Notoriety is the short glory a man gets for doing what he ought to be ashamed of.

Notoriety blows its own horn — the world blows the horn of reputation.

Novelty

If you want to take the starch out of a novelty, just set it to work at something useful.

Obstinacy

There are two kinds of obstinacy: obstinacy in the right and obstinacy in the wrong. One is the strength of a great mind and the other is the strength of a little one.

Old Age

I have never know a person to live to 110, or more, and then died, to be remarkable for anything else.

A genial old man is pleasant to look upon, but a frisky old man is too much like an Irish wake to be captivating.

One of the privileges of old age seems to be to give advice that nobody will follow and relating experiences that everybody mistrusts.

Opinions

Opinions are worth just about as much as turnips are — when there is a big crop of turnips.

When we are young we change our opinions too often; when we are old, too seldom.

Opinions should be formed with great caution and changed with greater.

"People of good sense" are those whose opinions agree with ours.

Opportunity

The reason good opportunity is so often lost is because most people are hunting for good circumstance.

Opportunities are game birds and must be got on the wing.

Originality

Originality in writing is as difficult as getting a fishpole by the side of a trout brook — all the good poles have been cut long ago.

About the most originality that any writer can hope to achieve honestly is to steal with good judgment.

Originators

Originators make fame, while imitators make the money.

Parsimony

Parsimony is the sentimentalism of avarice while economy is the logic of common sense.

Passions

Men will believe their passions quicker than their conscience, and yet their passions are generally wrong and their conscience generally right.

Just about in proportion that the passions are weak men are virtuous.

Patience

Patience, if it is merely constitutional, doesn't have any more virtue than cold feet do.

The best thing I know of to try a man's patience is a kicking heifer. If he finds himself praying for the heifer every time she kicks, he has got patience of the heart and brain both.

It ain't but little trouble for a graven image to be patient, not even in fly time.

Peace

It is a curious fact that mankind in hunting for peace has started all of the trouble that the world has ever seen.

Pedant

A pedant is one who fills himself in the cellar with clam broth of literature and then picks his teeth in the society of the learned.

A pedant is a very learned individual who mistakes a popgun for a pistol.

Pedantry is a little knowledge on parade.

Pedigrees

If I was starving, I wouldn't hesitate to swap off all the

pedigree I had, and all my relations had, for a bowl of pottage, and throw in two great-grandfathers into the bargain.

The only pedigree worth transmitting is goodness, and that is the very thing that cannot be transmitted.

PETS

A pet lamb always makes a cross ram.

PHILOSOPHY

Philosophy is born in the head and dies in the heart.

Philosophy is the art of making ourselves happy, but yet I find 7 times as much philosophy in the world as I do happiness.

All the philosophy in the world won't make a hard trotting horse ride easy, but it teaches how to make the jolts average.

You may live *by* philosophy but you can't live *on* it.

A philosopher is a person who is great in bilious colic — provided somebody else has got the colic.

Philosophy has no power to create happiness or annul misery, but it can arrange the flowers on the bush so that the thorns are better hidden.

PINHEADS

A man with a very small head is like a pin without any — very apt to get into things beyond his depth.

PIOUS

I have known men so pious that when they went fishing on Sunday they always prayed for good luck.

Pity

About half our pity is satisfaction that it ain't our horse that has his leg broke.

Man pities his neighbor's misfortunes by calling them judgments from heaven.

Pleasure

Pleasure is like a hornet — generally ends with a sting.

Pleasures make folks *acquainted* with each other but it takes trials and grief to make them *know* each other.

Poetry

Poetry is the harmony of ideas.

Poetry is like honesty — you can't get an average on it. There is no such thing as poetry that is worth 50 cents on the dollar.

Poetry is a good deal like a clothesline — very apt to spread lengthways if at all.

Point of View

Every thing has two sides to it — and a square thing four.

Politeness

The rich should remember that when they reach heaven they will find Lazarus there and have to be polite to him.

Next to money — you can travel farther from home, and get back on, politeness than on any commodity I know of.

Politeness is the science of getting down on your knees before folks without getting your pants dirty.

Politeness is like lighting another man's candle by yours.

POLITICS

I have seen plenty of people who could set down at a corner grocery and run the morals and politics of the whole country with perfect precision, who couldn't get credit of the proprietor for another glass of whiskey to save their lives.

Politics is the apology of plunder.

The role of the political demagogue is to induce others to beat the bush, while he coolly bags the rabbit.

The tongue is a very fast member of the body politic — it does all the talking and two thirds of the thinking.

The politician is as limber as the figger U. It can stand on her head, or her feet, or lay down on her side, and be the same thing all the time. It can turn a somerset backwards, or back a somerset forwards.

If you want to find out how mean and dishonest you have always been, get a nomination and run for some office.

There is a great difference between holding a high office or having a high office hold you.

When a man swaps horses we know he does it for gain, but when he changes his politics or religion we are at a loss to tell whether he is influenced by policy or principle.

POSSESSIONS

Men value things before they have got them and after

they have lost them more than they do when they have got them.

If mankind could only take their possessions with them the world would have been impoverished ages ago.

POVERTY

Poverty is the only birthright that a man can't lose.

Confess your sorrows, fears, hopes, loves and even your deviltry to men, but don't let them get a smell of your poverty — poverty has no friends, not even among the paupers.

POWER

Power either makes a man a tyrant or a tool.

It would hardly do to trust an angel with absolute power.

PRAISE

To praise in others what you would like to have praised in you is merely blowing your own trumpet.

Our continuous desire for praise ought to satisfy us of our mortality, if nothing else will.

PRAYER

There is a good deal of praying and swearing that is alike — the parties don't mean anything by what they say.

The time to pray is not when we are in a tight spot, but just as soon as we get out of it.

PREACHING

The world is choked up with human beings, who have

either got to be scared or drove into heaven, if they ever get there.

PRECEPTS

Precepts are good but endorsed by example they are more negotiable.

Bringing a young one up on precepts is like sending him down in the cellar without a candle to learn him to see in the dark.

Precept is the bucksaw; *experience* the elbow grease that runs the cussed thing.

There is just as much difference between precept and example as there is between a horn that blows a noise and one that blows a tune.

PREJUDICE

Prejudice is a house plant that is apt to wither if you take it outdoors among folks.

PREPAREDNESS

Blessed is he who always carries a big stone in his hand but never heaves it.

There are 2 things in this life for which we are never fully prepared, and that is twins.

PRIDE

A man who ain't got any pride is like a dog who ain't got any strength to his tail.

There is no such a thing as being proud before humans and humble before God.

Pride and poverty have traveled together about 5000

years and pretend to love each other, but they can't fool anybody but themselves.

PROGRESS

Progress seems to be the ideal of creation, but all progress seems to end in destruction rather than perfection.

PROOF

I have finally come to the conclusion that if I can't prove a thing without betting 5 dollars on it, the thing's got a dreadful weak spot somewhere.

PROPHECY

Don't never prophesy, for if you prophesy wrong, nobody will forget it, and if you prophesy right, nobody will remember it.

If you must prophesy, or spoil, prophesy good and clever things. It is just as cheap, just as likely to happen, and more creditable to you.

If a man ain't got nothing to do, and can't find anything to do, prophesying is a good business for him to go into.

PROVERB

There is no place to hide in a good proverb. One word too much will weak it, one word too weak will spoil it.

PRUDES

Prudes are coquettes gone to seed.

Prudery seems to me nothing more than modesty tired out.

Punctuality

A man who always *misses* the train by getting there 10 minutes too soon don't never seem to get left.

Punishment

A boy never feels half so good as when he is spanked and sot away to cool.

Punishment, to hit the spot,
Should be few but red-hot.

In whipping a young one, you don't never ought to stop till you get clean through.

When I was a boy I had rather be licked twice than postponed once.

Reading

He who reads and don't reflect is like the one who eats and don't exercise.

Mankind reads too much and learns too little.

Reason

Nature gave man reason and showed him how to use it, but man loves to open the throttle and let reason hum. This accounts for his running off from the track so often and getting bust up.

Reciprocity

Don't do for others what you wouldn't think of asking them to do for you.

Reflection

The man who has learned to reflect has laid by something nice for a wet day.

REINCARNATION

Most folks think if they were to live their lives over again, they would be *different,* but I have never heard any of them propose to live *better.*

RELATIVES

He who lends money to his relatives becomes a debtor rather than a creditor.

RELIGION

I never could see any use making wooden gods male or female.

I like a wide-awake Christian — one whose virtue has some cayenne pepper in it.

Men seem to be to be divided into slow Christians and wide-awake sinners.

People are more apt to make a shield of their religion than a pruning hook.

Where religion is a trade, morality is a merchandise.

Sectarian religion is like cider drawn from a musty cask — it always tastes like the cask.

Those who enter heaven may find the outer walls plastered with creeds, but they won't find any on the inside.

There is a great deal of religion in this world that is like a life preserver — only put on at the moment of extreme danger, and put on then, half the time, hind side before.

I wouldn't give a shilling a pound for religion that you can't take anywhere out into the world with you, even to a horse race, if you have a mind to, without losing it.

There are lots of folks who are in such a hurry to get

religion that they confess sins they ain't guilty of and overlook those that they are.

Pure religion is like good old hyson tea: it cheers but don't intoxicate.

Whenever a minister has preached a sermon that pleases the whole congregation he probably has preached one that the Lord won't endorse.

Before you undertake to change a man's politics or religion be sure you have got a better one to offer.

You can't show me a country that has existed yet where the people, all of them, professed one religion and persecuted all other kinds but what the religion ruined the country.

If a preacher can't strike oil boring 40 minutes, he has either got a poor gimlet or else he is boring in the wrong place.

Religion was never designed as a business but to regulate and correct business with.

Repentance

Most people repent of their sins by thanking God they ain't so wicked as their neighbors.

The best way I know of to repent of anything is to do better next time.

Confess your sins to the Lord and you will be forgiven; confess them to man and you will be laughed at.

It is a good thing for those who have been sinful to turn over a new leaf, but it often happens that, in doing this, they turn over two leaves at once and become so suddenly virtuous that they freeze stiff.

It is much easier to repent of sins that we have committed than to repent of those which we intend to commit.

It is dreadful easy to repent of other people's sins — but not very profitable.

There are many people who repent of their sins simply to clear the way for a fresh lot.

A lot of repentance consists of hiding our sins from ourselves and exposing them to our neighbors.

Reputation

A man is always stronger while he is making a reputation than he is after it is made.

Reputation is what the world *thinks* of us; character is what the world *knows* of us.

No man ever yet increased his reputation by contradicting lies.

Revenge

Revenge holds the cup to the lips of another but drinks the dregs itself.

Rhetoric

Rhetoric is often mistaken for eloquence — there is as much difference as between an old-fashioned Fourth of July oration and a little child's rehearsal of the Lord's Prayer.

Riches

No man is rich who wants any more than what he has got.

Riches take wings and fly out of sight — and I have known them to take the proprietor with them.

RIPE

As soon as a peach gets ripe it starts to rot.

RUMOR

Rumor is like a swarm of bees — the more you fight them the less you get rid of them.

Rumor is a spark, then a fire, then a conflagration, and then ashes.

SAFETY

It is the safest thing to let every man kick his own dog.

SARCASM

True sarcasm is in the point, not in the shaft, of the arrow.

Sarcasm is an undertaker in tears.

The most bitter sarcasm sleeps in silent words.

SATIRE

Satire is a cruel weapon, but in malicious hands the handle is more dangerous than the blade.

SCIENCE

Science is the literature of truth.

SECRETS

If you circulate secrets, you lose them, and if you keep them you lose the interest on the investment.

Secrets are a mortgage on friendship.

He who does a good thing secretly steals a march on heaven.

Sectarianism

I wouldn't undertake to correct a man's sectarian views any quicker than I would tell him which road to take at a corner when I didn't know myself which was the right one.

Self

The world pays us what it owes us oftener than we pay what we owe the world.

The surest way to be remembered after we are dead is to remember others while we are alive.

The more a man talks about himself, the more he is apt to lie about his neighbors.

Most people miss their average by weighing themselves on their own scales instead of the neighbor's.

I don't never have any trouble in regulating my own conduct, but to keep other folks straight is what bothers me.

What a blessed thing it is that we can't "see ourselves as others see us" — the sight would take all the starch out of us.

However cunning you may be, the easiest man for you to cheat is yourself.

When a man gets talking about himself he seldom fails to be eloquent and often reaches the sublime.

We mingle in society not so much to meet others as to escape ourselves.

After trying for 35 years to have my own way in all things I have finally come to the conclusion to split the difference.

SENTIMENTALIST

A sentimentalist is one who trades in sentiment more for the poetry he thinks he sees in it than the truth.

SHREWDNESS

The shrewd people are those who think as they please, and act to suit others.

SILENCE

You can listen a flippant talker into silence in one half of the time you can subdue him any other way.

The man who can't hold his tongue can't steer it well.

When a man ain't got anything to say that's the best time to say it.

Silence is one of the hardest arguments to refute.

Silence makes but few blunders and those it can correct.

Talk little and listen loud is the way to make others suspect you know a great deal more than you actually do.

I have known many a man to beat in an argument by just nodding his head once in a while and simply say, "Just so, just so."

It is hard to find a man of good sense who can look back upon any occasion and wish he had said some more, but it is easy to find many who wish they had said less.

A thing said is hard to recall but unsaid it can be spoken any time.

Brevity is the child of silence and is a great credit to the old man.

SIMPLICITY

The great strength of simplicity lays in the words, *not in the ideas.*

SIN

I suppose one reason why the "road to ruin" is broad is to accommodate the great amount of travel going in that direction.

There are lots of folks in this world who can keep nine out of the Ten Commandments without any trouble, but the one that is left they can't keep the small end of.

The hardest sinner in the whole lot to convert is the one who spends half of his time in sinning and the other half in repentance.

I had rather have a wide-awake sinner, for every purpose, than a half-dead saint.

SKEPTIC

A skeptic is one who knows too much to be a good fool and too little to be wise.

SLANDER

Slander travels on the wind and where it comes from and where it goes, nobody knows.

Slander is like the tin kettle tied to a dog's tail — a very good kind of kettle so long as it ain't our dog's tail.

If you can't kill slander dead the first time, like a hornet, you had better not strike it.

Smiles

My tears are private property; my smiles belong to the world.

Society

Society is burning on an altar natural rights and then sacredly watching the ashes.

Solitude

The man who is fit to live in solitude is the one that society can't spare.

Solitude is a thickly settled place full of memories.

Sophist

A sophist is a man who puts his light under a half-bushel for the sake of letting the light shine through the cracks.

Sorrow

The only play philosophers can offer us to get rid of our sorrows is to grin and bear them.

Don't parade your sorrows before the world, but bury them as the dog does his old bones, and then growl if any-body offers to dig them up.

Speaking

What I say is instant, and I can't alter it. I can't sit down, or stand up, and study a thing out any more than I can sit down and think how to lift a ton.

Speculation

There is a great deal of speculation that is trying to un-twist the untwistable. This is just about as smart as sitting down in a washtub, taking hold of the handles, and trying to lift the unliftable.

START

You can find two men who know the right time to start to one who knows when the right time is to stop.

STEALING

Stealing is the oldest sin on record — stealing apples.

STOMACHE-ACHE

Heaven bless the stomach-ache. If it wasn't for it many a deacon wouldn't have a good excuse for hot rum.

STUBBORNNESS

When stupidity and stubbornness join we have a man who is only fit for a snubbing post.

SUCCESS

The two most successful insects are the ant and the hornet — one trusts to industry and patience, and the other to nerve and dispatch. Take your choice, Gentlemen!

When five men call you a success and one man a failure, the one man's testimony is what fetches the jury.

Rise early, work hard and late, live on what you can't sell, give nothing away, and if you don't die rich and go to the devil, you may sue me for damages.

Diogenes was a greater man than Alexander not because he lived in a tub but because a tub was all he wanted to live in — wealth could not flatter him nor poverty make him afraid.

The man who thinks he can't do it, is always more than half right.

Swearing

Swearing is the metallic currency of loafers.

A boy will learn to swear well in just half the time that it takes to learn the Ten Commandments.

Taxes

If you would escape envy, abuse and taxes, you must live in a deep well and only come out in the nighttime.

Temper

A man who mistakes his surly temper for superior intelligence is like a toothless cur who got whipped in his last fight and is going to get licked in his next one.

Temperance

We have four kinds of temperance people — those who are temperate from principle; those who have no appetite to gratify; those who have not the money to buy whiskey with; and, those who have the money but only drink at somebody else's expense.

Temptation

The weakest of all men is the man who has never been tempted — and thinks he can't be!

Theories

Theories are good if you navigate them, but if you let them navigate you, beware of the lee shore.

Tomorrow

Tomorrow is a good day to die in — but for business purposes it don't compare to today.

Total Depravity

I don't believe in total depravity — unless a man has a good chance.

Trouble

The highest rate of interest we pay is on borrowed trouble.

Trust

He who is willing to trust everybody is willing to be cheated by everybody.

Truth

Truth can speak for itself but a lie must have an interpreter.

Truth is a citizen of the world; it has no pedigree, and is the same in all languages.

As scarce as truth is the supply has always been greater than the demand.

Truth can take its time but a lie has to get up and get.

It is the untrue things which we discard, as well as the true things which we accept, which educate us.

Truth is radical; fiction is conservative.

Truth is said to be stranger than fiction — *it is to most folks!*

Error will slip through a crack while truth will get stuck in the doorway.

Vanity

The world has no wind to spare to blow up the bladder of your vanity — it needs what it has for its own.

Vanity has a ravenous appetite and a remorseless digestion.

Rather than be out of a job, vanity will brag of its vices.

Vice

Before a vice can become very dangerous it has got to become respectable.

When vice is put in a package for the market it is always marked "VIRTUE" outside.

Virtue

The man who can't find any virtue in the human heart has probably given us a faithful synopsis of his own.

If virtue did not so often manage to make herself repulsive vice would not be half so attractive.

Virtue don't consist in the absence of passions but in the control of them.

Virtue is like strength — a man can't tell how much he has until he comes across something he can't lift.

Waiting

This settling down and folding our arms and waiting for something to turn up, is about as rich a speculation as going out into a 400-acre lot, setting down on a sharp stone, with a pail between our knees, and waiting for a cow to back up and be milked.

WANTS

He who buys what he can't want will ere long want what he can't buy.

We are poor not from what we need, but from what we want.

WEALTH

Wealth is baggage at the owner's risk.

The wealth of a person should be estimated not by the amount he has but by the use he makes of it.

WEATHER-WISE

People who are very weather-wise are not very otherwise.

WHISKEY

Whiskey is a hard thing to convince, therefore I never argue with a drunken man.

WIDOWER

There are no weeds that wilt so quick as the weeds of a widower.

WIDOWS

If you don't mean business, my boy, beware of the widows.

When you court a widow do it with spurs on.

WISDOM

If you seek wisdom study men and things; if you desire learning study the dictionary.

Wisdom is as old as creation; learning is in its swaddling clothes.

Some folks as they grow older grow wise, but most folks simply grow stubborner.

Wisdom don't consist in knowing more that is new, but in knowing less that is false.

Wit

There is this difference between wit and humor: wit makes you think, humor makes you laugh.

Conversation should be enlivened with wit — not composed of it.

Witty speeches are like throwing stones at a target — the more time spent in taking aim, the less danger there is in hitting the mark.

Men of great wit may be compared to a great fire, you can't get near enough to it to get warm without getting burnt.

It is time enough for a man to laugh at his own wit after others get through.

Wives

It is easy enough for a man to pick out a good wife for another man — he always picks out the one he don't want for himself.

Women

Woman holds the balance of power, and it is lucky for the rest of the world she don't know it.

When a woman gets going downhill she don't want to stop — even at the bottom.

There is nothing like a woman's wit to get a man into a tight spot — or to get him out of it.

Woman's influence is powerful — especially when she wants something.

Woman has no friendships. She either loves, despises, or hates.

No woman was ever satisfied to be a prude who could be a successful flirt.

Woman beat the first man born into the world out of a dead-sure thing, and she can beat the last one with the same cards.

Tongue-tied women are very scarce and very valuable.

The strongest propensity in woman's nature is to want to know what's going on, the next strongest is to boss the job.

Man without woman would be as stupid a game as playing checkers alone.

Words

It is uncommon hard to annihilate a man with words — although it is often undertook.

Words are often seen hunting for an idea, but an idea is never seen hunting for words.

Work

There is one great advantage in wearing out instead of rusting out — the last six inches of the man who wears out is as bright as the first was.

Writing

There is quite a difference between a *lu*minous writer

and a *volu*minous writer, although many confound the two.

It would be safe to brand all of the original literature that has wandered around for thousands of years — "strayed or stolen."

Original writers are scarce, but those that can steal with good judgment are scarcer.

Yankee

If you trade with a Yankee, steal his jackknife first, for if he gets to whittling you are gone in spite of thunder.

Zeal

Zeal and folly are twins — only zeal was born a little first.

Zeal in religion is the way that bigots are made, and zeal in selling dry goods is the way that good liars are made.

CHAPTER TEN

Uncle Josh's New Year's Resolutions

"To avoid all troubles of lawsuits from heirs I have decided to administer my own estate by spending it."

That I won't smoke any more cigars, only at somebody else's expense.

That I won't borrow nor lend — especially lend.

That I will live within my income, if I have to get trusted to do it.

That I will be polite to everybody, except mosquitoes and bed bugs.

That I won't advise anybody, until I know the kind of advice they are anxious to follow.

That I won't wear any more tight shoes, if I have to go barefoot to do it.

That I won't eat any more chicken soup with a one-tined fork.

That I won't swap dogs with no man, unless I can swap two for one.

That I won't object to any man on account of his color, unless he happens to be blue.

That I won't swear any, unless I am put under oath.

That I won't believe in total depravity, only in gin at 4 shillings a gallon.

That poverty may be a blessing, but if it is, it is a blessing in disguise.

That I will take my whiskey hereafter straight—straight to the gutter.

That the world owes me a living—provided I earn it.

That I will stick to my tailor as long as he sticks to me.

That I won't swap any horses with a deacon.

That no man shall beat me in politeness, not so long as politeness continues to be as cheap as it is now.

That I won't have any religious creed myself, but will respect everybody else's.

That if a lovely woman smacks me on one cheek, I will turn her the other also.

That if a man calls me a fool, I won't ask him to prove it.

That I will lead a moral life, even if I lose a good deal of fun by it.

That if a man tells me a mule won't kick, I will believe what he says without trying it.

That if anybody loses even a goose I will weep with him, for it is a tough business to lose a goose.

That if I can get a hen that can lay 2 eggs a day, I shall insist upon her keeping one of the eggs on hand for a sinking fund.

That it is no disgrace to be bit by a dog unless he does it the second time.

That one of the riskiest things to straddle is the back of a 60-day note.

That the best time to repent of a blunder is just before the blunder is made.

That I will try hard to be honest, but it will be just my darn luck to miss it.

That I won't grow any cats. Spontaneous cats have killed the business.

That I will love my mother-in-law if it takes all the money I can earn to do it.

That I will respect public opinion just as long as I can respect myself doing it.

That when I hear a man bragging on his ancestors, I won't envy him, but I will pity the ancestors.

That I won't believe in any ghost or ghostess unless they weigh about 140 pounds and can eat a good square meal.

That I won't bet on nothing, for things that require betting on lack something.

That I will brag on my wife all the time, but I will do it silently.

That I won't be surprised at anything, not even to be told that Ben Franklin was a spendthrift, or that Lazarus died rich.

That I will despise most things that I see, not out of malice but out of wisdom.

That I won't hanker for happiness, but if I see any that I think is a bargain I will shut up one eye and go for it.

That I won't wish I was as pure as King David, but that I was purer than I am.

That I won't covet any man's wife, nor his oxen, nor his cornstalks, nor the color of his mustache.

That I will laugh every good chance I can get, whether it makes me grow fat or not.

Finally, I will search for things that are little, for things that are lonesome, avoiding all torchlight processions, bands of brass music, women's rights conventions and grass widows generally.

CHAPTER ELEVEN

Uncle Josh's Cook Book

"Lo and behold!
The Lord sends us meat,
But the Devil sends us Cooks!"

October 15th, 1880

To the Dear Public:

The Receipts for cooking which appear in this little volume are not to be considered arbitrary; they are the suggestions of a man who never has been able to cook his own goose just exactly right, but rest assured, my dear friends, that they are submitted to your consideration by one who has but little malice in his nature and less cunning.

Should none of them be found to work perfection, don't tear the hair out of your head about it; baldness won't improve the matter. Just thank the Lord they ain't any worse than they are, and you have gained something by the experiment.

How to Construct Cranberry Pie

Roll out 2 thin covers of dough; lay one of them in an earthern dish, with the bottom down; deposit a pint of cooked cranberries on the top of the bottom cover; spread the other cover on top of the cranberries; lacerate a few holes in the upper side of the top cover to let the steam meander; cast the pie into the oven; let it stew for 27 minutes by the clock; then twitch it out; set it in a draft to chill; serve it up with some brandy or rum-cheese; cut the pie acrost the top, into two halfs; give one half to your wife and children and mother-in-law; take the other half yourself, observing that poor Pa is sick and cranberry pie always did agree with him.

Roast Goose

Pick out a tender goose (if you can); dispel the feathers from his person carefully; amputate his head and feet; remove him internally; make a filling of high seasoned dough; sew him up tight; lay him in an iron pan, face side up; insert him into a hot place; let him try it for 4 hours; flop him over once in a while, to get an average on him; jab him occasionally with a 3-tined fork, to see what he is a-doing; when you think he has got through, snatch him out; lay him on a platter; surround his person with dandelions and sweet majoram; let two people eat him — one goose is not quite enough for two people, but is a little too much for one.

How to Devil Crabs

The art of deviling crabs is a joyful one, but it is yet in its infancy, and possibly ought to remain there. But we are in full possession of the art, in all its primeval force and beauty, and will send a knowledge of the same upon receipt of 25 cents, and warrant the receipt, or return the money by the next mail, and throw in dozen crabs besides. For full particulars address, Josh Billings, Paragrapher, care of G. W. Carleton and Co., Publishers, book and stationery dealers, corner of 5th Avenue and 23d St., underneath 5th Avenue Hotel, near Madison Park, city, and state of New York, United States of America, Western Hemisphere.

Yours with delight,
JOSH BILLINGS

New York, August 9th, 1880

DEAR MADAM:

You say you have tried my receipt, received by mail, for "Deviling Crabs," and it wouldn't work. This astounds me; I never knew it to hesitate before.

Please state (at my expense) the exact size of the crabs you tried it on; the number of claws he had; whether he was a hard-shell or a soft-shell; about how old he might be; also what your impressions were about the natural disposition of the crab; whether he was particularly warlike, or docile in his manners; and any facts that may occur to you. An explicit answer to the above interrogatory will enable me to get at a diagnosis of this particular crab's case.

Yours politely,
JOSH BILLINGS

HASH

Hash is made out of castoff vittles, homogeneous, abnormal, and at times unique in its nature. Hash has done more to push the human family than any other kind of mixed food.

It is impossible to lay down any specific rule to create this abstruse and at the same time gentle food. Anything that will chop fluently will produce hash. No one has taken out a patent yet, for the production of this promiscuous viand.

Hash requires but little cooking, but may be compared to a foundered horse — goes the best when it is well warmed up.

For the creation of hash, talent is of more importance than genius.

Finally, hash may be likened unto the human family — from some standpoints it is fair, from others it is bad, and from all suspicious.

How to Make Shadow Soup

Pick out a good thin chicken (Shanghai breed is the best); disrobe him of his plumage; amputate his spurs; remove the comb from his head; confiscate his tail feathers; place him in a strong sunlight; let the shadow reach across two gallons of strained rain water in a shallow pan; let the shadow remain on the surface of the water for 10 minutes; then take him by the bill and lead him gently backwards and forwards through the water, three or four times; bring the water to a sudden boil; season to suit the taste and serve up with a raw onion and a bunch of wooden toothpicks.

This soup is very popular with boarding-house keepers,

and it is said will cure the dyspepsia, or kill the patient, I have forgot which.

To Make a Good Rum Sauce

Take one quart of good old New England rum, or brandy, or whiskey; toss into it six ounces of sweet Orange County butter; mingle slices of lemon with it; dust it with nutmeg; chastise it severely with "A" Number 1 white sugar; bring it to a mild boil on a hot stove; stir it resolutely while boiling; taste of it often to see if it has got the right idea to it; take it off carefully from the stove; let it drip slowly into a gilt-edge earthen bowl; set it away gently for two hours in an icebox, to equalize; then use it freely on baked, boiled, or fried puddings, in quantities to flatter the taste.

A wineglass of this elixir, taken before meals, as a brace, is not a difficult thing to struggle with, but it is designed principally for puddings.

Pine Grove, Indiana
September 5th, 1880

Dear Josh:

I have tried, in my household, your great remedy for making "Good Rum Sauce," and must say that nothing has ever entered our family, since it was organized, that has given such distinguished satisfaction.

Joshua, you are a philosopher and philanthropist; may you never grow bald-headed. You won't need any tombstone when you die; your epitaph will be a household word. "Rum Sauce" has done the business for you.

Enclosed please find 10 dollars, and put it to the credit of "Rum Sauce" on your books. My wife uses the sauce on all her pudding fixings, and I take it regular, before meals, as an alterative.

Yours sweetly,

Bob Wagstaff, Jun.

Fried Eels

Bait a hook with the toe of an old Indian rubber shoe; cast the hook into some mudhole where the eels congregate; when the eel bites, twitch as though you had been stung by a hornet, drag the eel home with the hook in his mouth; boil him in hot water for 60 minutes to loosen his skin; peel him as you would a banana; then soak him in kerosene oil and turpentine, equal parts, for four days, to quell his muscular actions; then cast him into a brass kettle; put him onto a red-hot stove, and let him fry until he gets enough of it; then coil him up in the bottom of a porcelain dish, like a piece of tarred rigging; then pour an ointment over him made of sour milk scented with cinnamon oil; then set him out on the front steps of your house; open the front gate wide; go to bed; and let somebody steal him.

To Make Doughnuts

Take one quart of rye flour and three pints of corn meal; amalgamate well together; sift them through a cane-bottomed chair; add six ounces of pork fat; and jam well together; lay the jam on a table and level it with an iron rolling pin until you get tired; turn it over and roll it again on the other side; sprinkle with a little molasses as you go along; cut it up into fractions 3 inches and a half long by 2 and a half wide; twist each fraction into the shape of a corkscrew; drop the fractions into some boiling tallow and let them sputter for 9 minutes; take them out with a pair of tongs; and lay them into a colander to drain, pack them down tight in a stone jar; and serve them up with cold water when the minister and his wife make their annual winter evening visit.

How to Cook a Shad

Catch the shad first; this is all important — many a shad has been cooked and eaten before he was catched — eradicate the scales from his adipose membrane; deftly remove the alimentary arrangements from his subterranean nature; banish all the bones from his being; stuff him with ground crackers lubricated with Scoharie County butter; perfume suitably with pepper and salt; straddle a gridiron with his person, over a golden mass of hickory coals, for 28 minutes; lay him on a milk-white platter, his head to the windward; surround him with sliced lemon and tuberoses; blow the horn for dinner and ask in some of your poor relations to the feast.

Shad eaten in this way will be blest, whether you ask grace or not.

Good Rye Coffee

Rye coffee is good, but Rio is better. To make good rye coffee, take one quart of old rye (not liquid rye, but rye in the berry); if you can't get rye, beans will do; burn it in a spider over hot coals until it is burnt; drop in a lump of possum fat and agitate it lively, while it is burning, with a pewter spoon; burn it until it is as black and shiny as patent leather; let it cool off, and then spill it into a coffee mill; grind it until it is ground; take a teacup of the grindings and boil it until it is boiled; insert sugar to the taste; whiten with good Ayrshire milk. This is a dose for two; drink standing to the success of the American flag, and the everlasting perpetuation of the Union, one and inseparable.

Hasty Pudding

Hasty pudding is made out of Injun meal and hot water, about half and half. It gets its name from the sudden manner in which it is made.

Hang a 4-gallon kettle on a crane, in an old-fashioned fireplace, fill it up to the waist with water, set her to boiling, then sift in the meal with one hand, and with a wooden ladle stir lively with the other; in 20 minutes it will be done; dip out into two quart bowls, half pudding and half milk; call the roll and let the young ones pitch in.

Two bowls full is a dose for a young one; when they have finished, wipe their mouths with a crash towel, kiss them all around, hear their little prayers, and tuck them up in their little beds for the night.

Chronology

Geese were first roasted during the 3rd century.

Roast pig was discovered about the year 896.

Boiled eggs were invented during the reign of Trajan.

Quails on toast appeared about the end of the 9th century.

The first mention made of baked shad was in 1493.

We have no earlier record of hash than the year 2.

Oysters were found in 756, appeared later, on the half shell, 804.

There is no positive date when the first Bologna sausage was seen; one historian says in the fore part of the 6th century, others put it later. I am more interested when the last one will appear than I am when the first one did.

Pumpkin Pie

Good old reliable pumpkin pie, one inch and a half deep, baked on a platter 16 inches in diameter, mingled with sweet cream and sugar, saturated with nutmeg, and done to a rich golden brown, the joy of our granddads, and the pride of our granddames, the schoolboy's luncheon, and the parson's desert, has departed, and left no recipe behind. The cunning of the hands that once made them is now still.

Carrots and squash, and sweet potatoes have drove dear old pumpkin pie out of existence; the places that knew it once, now know it no more.

When I think of these things, my heart grows sad and lonesome.

Pickled Tongue

Take a good quiet tongue (there are a great many tongues that won't keep still long enough to pickle); thrust the tongue into boiling water for 7 minutes; peel it as you would a boiled potato; prepare a fluid of vinegar, spiced with cloves and cardamon seeds; put the tongue in a glass jar, with the round side of the tongue up; pour the solution slowly over the tongue; set it away where the rats can't get at it; some lonesome night, when the bleak winds of November are mourning outside, eat the tongue all alone by yourself; wash it down with a cup of strong coffee; then go to bed; and somewhere about the center of night you will see your late lamented mother-in-law prancing around the room, a 2:40 gait, on a cream-colored nightmare.

The Noble Codfish Ball

Come listen to my story, ye men and women all,
While I sing to you a ditty of the Noble Codfish Ball.
Corn beef and cabbage has its friends, and so has succotash,
And some there be who relish a plate of mutton hash.
Baked beans and pork are well enough, but since poor Adam's fall,
Nothing has discounted yet, a boneless codfish ball.
Let Britons praise roast beef, and Frenchmen frogs' hind legs,
And Germans sing of sausages, and beer in little kegs,
The universal Yankee nation, her lads and lasses all,
Will ever shout the praises of the Noble Codfish Ball.

Roast Clam

Roast clam is joy on the half shell, glory enough for one day, as natural as an infant, and as luscious as honey in the comb.

Take a Rockaway clam; lay it softly on the glittering

coals; watch the bivalve with the solicitude of a mother; when it opens its steaming mouth, and issues from its lips the exquisite aroma, lift it delicately to the platter; unhinge its upper cover; drop a wee lump of butter on the liquid morsel; salt and pepper the dear viand gently; raise it up tenderly with the left hand; part your mustache with the right; throw your head back as though you was inspired; drop the juicy mass into your mouth; wink languidly; swallow slowly; and the joyful victory is complete. Three cheers!!! for roast clam on the half shell.

Conclusions

Having examined closely all the different kinds of cooking, boiling, roasting and stewing, from quails on toast, all the way down to hash on a platter; having eaten in all the famous restaurants in the country, paying 5 dollars for the chance; and having dined in 10-cents saloons, on one kind of meat and two kinds of turnips; having studied bills of fare until I lost my appetite in a labyrinth of miserable French, I feel like shouting, with the epicure of old, "The Lord sends us meat, but the Devil sends us cooks."

CHAPTER TWELVE

Uncle Josh Bids You a Fond Adieu

Josh never quit writing with the same pungent wit nor ever lost his zest for travel. Although he stopped doing the Allminax *in 1880, he kept up his column in the* New York Weekly *and in the* Century Magazine *until his death. He also continued doing lectures although the last few years he gave them sitting down. But most of all he loved his grandchildren. He wrote:*

I have got grandchildren and they are worse than the first crop to riot among the feelings.

The grandpa is an individual, aged somewhere between 50 and one hundred years, of a promiscuous temperament, and is a common occurrence in all well-regulated families. Next to a healthy mother-in-law, they have more active business on hand than any other party in the household.

They are the standard authority on all leading topics, and what they don't know about things that took place 65 years ago, or will take place for the next 65 years to come, is a damage for anyone to know.

Grandpas are not entirely useless. They are handy to hold babies and feed the pigs and are very smart at mending a broken broom handle, sifting coal ashes, and putting clothes on the line on washdays.

I have seen grandpas that could churn good, but I consider it a mighty mean trick to set an old fellow of 80 years to churning butter. I am a grandpa myself, but I won't churn butter for no concern, not if I understand myself. I am as solid on this conclusion as a graven image. I am willing to rock baby all the time while the womenfolks are boiling soap; I am willing to cut rags, to work up into rag carpets; they can keep me hunting hens' eggs wet days or picking green currants; I will even dip candles or core apples for sauce or turn a grindstone; but, by thunder, I won't churn. I have examined myself on this subject and I will bet a jacknife, so long as he remains in his right mind, Josh Billings won't churn.

As a general thing grandpas are a set of conceited old fools who don't seem to realize that what they know themselves is the result of experience and that younger people have got to get their knowledge the same way. Grandpas are poor help at bringing up children; they have got precept and catechism enough, but the young ones all seem to understand that Grandpa minds them a heap more than they mind Grandpa.

Like most grandpas he also looked with nostalgia at the days of yore — the good old days:

In ancient days, men, after considering an enterprise, proceeded with energy to execute it; now they shut up one eye and "pitch in."

In old times, if their judgment sanctioned, they considered the chances; now, they "let her rip."

Then, they drank moderately of water and brandy; now, they smile aqua fortis and suck sweet-scented turpentine through a quill.

Then, if circumstances made it imperative, they closed their business by effecting an honorable compromise; now, they "cave in," "squeal," or "absquat."

Then, contrary opinions were occasionally supported with reasonable wagers; now, every man "bets his pile" or "bottom dollar."

Then, most families held from 6 to 10 healthy children, within its hallowed circle a radiant mother, and a stalwart sire; now, too often a puny father with uncertain knees, a romantic madam with a pale lily at her breast, a wet nurse, 2 Bridgets and a kennel of sore-eyed pups.

Then, they went to meeting, to hear a doctrine sermon, and be humble before God; now, they flaunt into holy palaces and pay out fortunes every year to lounge on velvet and hear the Bible amateured by a dainty gentleman who handles their sins as he would a sleeping infant.

Then, our halls of legislature were filled with honest patriots; now, with clever bandits, whose courtesies dwell upon the tips of bowie knives and whose eloquence and arguments are resting in the chambers of deadly revolvers.

Then, we had youths apprenticed to an honest calling, whose indentures were diplomas; now, pale young gentlemen, emulous of physic or the law, who are pendant to the purlieus of the courts and colleges, watching for the falling of a crumb.

Then, we had maidens until they had been looked upon by at least 20 summers and were modest enough to pick out a husband from a score of earnest and honest men, whose very eyes had the promise of bread in them; now, 15 summers make a woman (or what we are obliged to take for one) and one so ripe, too, that he who first shakes the bush, gets the eager fruit.

Then our literature and learning was drawn from sound philosophy or quaint proverbs of sense, and the few books that prevailed were good; now, everybody writes a book, and every fool reads it; learning is stereotyped and wisdom is only 12 shillings a volume.

Then, industry created wants, virtue tempered them, and frugality supplied them; now, luxury has taken the place of industry, pride the place of virtue, and extravagance the place of frugality.

Then, men were solicitous about their characters; now, about their pedigrees.

Then, they found health at home; now, they hunt for it by travel.

Finally — if our grandpops should come among us with the plans and precepts of a hundred years ago, we, in our impudence and wickedness, would be caught laughing at them, while they, in virtuous sorrow, would be in tears over us, and thus would be enacted the scenes which always ensues when fools and sages meet.

How I do long (once in a while) for them good old days. Them days when the sun didn't rise before breakfast. Them days when there was more fun in 30 cents than there is now in 7 dollars and a half. Them days when a man married 145 pounds of woman and less than 9 pounds (all told) of anything else.

How I long for them good old days when education consisted in what a man did well. Them days when deacons was as austere as horse-radish and ministers preached to men's souls instead of their pockets. Them days when politics was the exception and honesty the rule.

How I do long for them good old days when lap dogs and wet nurses warn't known, and when brown bread and baked goose made a good dinner. Them days when a man who wasn't busy was watched, and when women spun only that kind of yarn that was good for darning of stockings.

How I do long for them good old days when now and then a gal baby was named Jerusha, and a boy wasn't spoilt if he was named Jeremiah.

All you who have tried the feathers and fuss of life, who have had the codfish of wealth, without sense, stuck under your nose, must long with me for them good old days when men were ashamed to be fools and women were ashamed to be flirts.

N.B. They used to make a milk punch in them days too, that was very handy to take.

So it was when Josh went back to the place of his childhood he could write:

Ah, it is pleasant; it is sad — to be back to the village of Pordunk. There are more people now there than there was when I was a boy, but how different are they! How different am I!

The old trees are the same. Man can't alter them. Goose Creek runs just where it did, with willows in all its elbows; the mountains on each side haven't grown any smaller, the birds sing the same songs, but I don't know anyone that I meet, and what is more lonesome, no one that I meet knows me.

When I go to Pordunk and want to see anybody that I remember, I go down the main street to the first corner, just where Joel Parker once lived, then I turn to the left, and keep on for a ways till I come to the little one-story church.

Just back of that they are all living now. They don't remember me when I go there, but I remember them.

It won't be very long now before I shall join them.

Uncle Josh died suddenly at Monterey, California, October 14, 1885, and was buried at Lanesboro, Massachusetts, his Pordunk.

Thank You

In general I want to thank the staffs of both the New York Public Library and the Library of Congress.

In particular my thanks to you, Williard Webb, for your splendid co-operative spirit. As chief of the Stack and Reader Division of the Library of Congress you have made my work on this book much easier. I want to thank also your assistant, Gordon Patterson, and Harold Cumbo, in charge of the study rooms, who has made my work so pleasant. And Benjamin Swenson, who has brought books to me almost before I needed them.

I also want to thank Clara Kent Pearce, whose splendid typing job was interspersed with solid criticism.

My best appreciation must go to the help that I got from Cyril Clemens's fine biography of Josh Billings. Like his famous kinsman, Mark Twain, he knows a good humorist and good humor when they happen along.

Finally, for this and for many other times, I want to express my heartfelt thanks to Franklin P. Meine of Chicago for the use of rare items from his magnificent humor collection which cannot be had anywhere else.